Staggering along with God

An Interview Biography

By Ellis Potter

Interviewer: Iszak Norbert

Edited by Peco Gaskovski

destinēe

© 2018 Ellis Potter

Without limiting the rights under copyright reserved above, no part of this publication may be reproduced, stored in, or introduced into a retrieval system, or transmitted in any form or by any means (electronic, mechanical, photocopying, or otherwise), without the prior written permission from the publisher, except where permitted by law, and except in the case of brief quotations embodied in critical articles and reviews. For information, write: info@destineemedia.com

Reasonable care has been taken to trace original sources and copyright holders for any quotations appearing in this book. Should any attribution be found to be incorrect or incomplete, the publisher welcomes written documentation supporting correction for subsequent printing.

Published by Destinée Media., www.destineemedia.com
Edited by Peco Gaskovski
Original Interviews by Izsák Norbert, 2017
Illustrations by Istvan Lente
Formatting by Istvan Szabo, Ifj.

Originally published in Hungarian as *Meredek görbén Istenhez*, by Harmat Publishing, Budapest

All rights reserved by the author.

ISBN: 978-1-938367-40-3

PART 1: A biography

Early life and family 6
The search for truth 23
Discovering Zen 30
Becoming a Christian 41
Life as a pastor 65
Life as a missionary 77
On teaching and lecturing 88

PART 2: Reflections and Insights

On storytelling and language 92
On prayer, meditation and making decisions 95
On culture 99
On faith, salvation and doubt 102
On music and art 108
On happiness and the fruits of the Spirit 117
On books, writing and sermons 124
On escapism and Heaven 130
On suffering and emotions 135
On apologetics 142
On words 144
Final thoughts 147

About Ellis Potter 150

PART 1
A biography

Early life and family

What are your first memories from childhood?

I believe that I remember nursing. I remember my mother saying to me: "I think you're ready for another birthday. I think you can be three." And I remember thinking: "Ah, then it's your mother's decision when you get to be three." That had to change. I had to figure out that it's actually the date that dictates this. But at first I thought your mother gave you your birthday. I also remember that my mother tried to teach me how to roller skate.

Tell me about your family.

My mother grew up in Los Angeles. Her name was Kathryn Matilda Gibson, and her mother was a descendant of Charles Wesley. Charles Wesley's daughter married an American man in Maryland named John Harper. My grandmother was the great-great granddaughter of this man.

My grandmother married a Swedish osteopath, whose name was Jetson. He came to America and was at Ellis Island for immigrant processing, where many people's names were changed to an Americanized spelling. They wrote his name as Gibson (his full name was Axel Emil Gibson). My grandparents came to California, to Los Angeles, and lived there for decades. There, my grandfather became a close friend of the famous occult writer Helena Blavatsky.

So your family had associations with both Wesley the Methodist and Blavatsky the occult writer?

Yes. I don't know how my grandparents met Blavatsky, but my grandfather was very interested in esotericism and was strongly connected with Hinduism. His medical practice as an osteopath was combined with examining patients' auras. He would have patients stand against a black screen, and would look at their aura—which he was gifted to see—and would say, "You have a malfunction of the liver", or whatever the diagnosis was, without any direct physical examination. He tended to be correct, and people came to see him. He had a good and profitable medical practice in the Bradbury building in downtown Los Angeles.

My grandmother was not strongly associated with Methodism, but attended a Filipino Presbyterian church near where they lived.

My grandparents had three children—my mother and her two older brothers. One of them became a radio and television personality. His name was Paul Gibson and he had his own show, the Paul Gibson Show. My other uncle, John, was a writer. He worked for magazines and made a good living.

Did your grandfather's friendship with Blavatsky or his esotericism have any influence on his family?

My mother told me that when she was five, she met Blavatsky. Blavatsky put her hand on my mother's head and said to my grandfather: "Name this child for me." My grandfather, because he was a doctor, had access to records and changed her birth certificate from Kathryn Matilda Gibson to Kathryn Matilda Blavatsky Gibson. I still have her birth certificate.

My grandfather wrote and published his own books, which were partly influenced by Blavatsky's worldview. He was very interested in diet, in the aura, the interface between the physical and non-physical parts of life and health, and things like that. In my family, there was never any question about the supernatural. I cannot remember a moment in my life when I was not a supernaturalist. I have always accepted that there are unseen personalities, influences and agencies that are connected with my life in various ways.

Your mother was renamed after Blavatsky, but did she believe in her teachings?

To some extent she did. She and my stepfather went to theosophical meetings, and also meetings of the Association for Research and Enlightenment of Edgar Cayce, an American philosopher. She was a Methodist in some sense as well.

Who did your mother marry?

A man by the name of Harold Rowe. I was named after my father's psychology professor and after his basketball coach at the University of Redlands—Dr. Ellis and Dr. Hoff. So, my name was Ellis Hoff Rowe. My parents soon divorced, and I had only brief contact with my father afterward. I was about one-and-a-half at the time, and as an immediate result of the stress of the divorce, I developed whooping cough. My father visited a couple of times, and I've seen a few letters that he wrote to my mother that mentioned me, but other than that, I had no contact with him in all my life. When he died, I didn't know it.

It's curious that you link the whooping cough to the stress of the divorce.

I do. I had the whooping cough bacteria, but I think my immune system was weak because of the stress of my parents divorcing, and all that tension. That seems quite logical to me. We lived in Redlands, California, and my mother had neighbors who were in the Methodist church. The neighbors were very friendly, and the mother of the family gave me daycare. She had three boys who were about my age and I was in their house a lot. These boys were really close friends, and this family was a great blessing to my mother. They attended a large church downtown, and soon my mother and I began to go with them. I remember Sunday school, learning the Lord's Prayer, singing songs, and things like that. It was quite a good experience.

Did having Charles Wesley as an ancestor have any influence on your mother's view of church or faith?

Not very much. But we did have Charles Wesley's Bible. I remember finding it on our bookshelves when I was a teenager. His own notes were written in that Bible, and the records of the birth of his children. It had the apocrypha in it too. It was a rather odd-shaped thick Bible that he carried in his saddlebag when he was on missionary trips in New England. My mother ultimately gave the Bible to the Wesleyan Museum, as she probably knew it had commercial value and didn't want her children to fight over it.

Did you spend the rest of your childhood in Redlands?

No. My mother got a better teaching job in a smaller town called Bloomington. We lived in a cottage on the street side of a

boysenberry farm. I had daycare again through a neighbor, in this case the mother of the family that owned and ran the farm. The mother's name was Mrs. Herbert, and the family was Mormon. Sometimes she took me to the Mormon stake for meetings and events, but I was never attracted to Mormonism. Living on a farm was quite interesting. There were fifteen acres of boysenberries, a cow, chickens, pigs, and rabbits. I saw pig-slaughtering when I was four. We ate the food from the farm, and everything was organic in terms of diet and lifestyle.

I have good memories of that, and I still have moderate organic tendencies in my own life. I grow a garden, make my own bread, and my own pickles. I think it's important for people to have contact with the earth, and to be physically engaged in what they eat to some extent. When my wife and I lived at L'Abri Fellowship in the Swiss Alps, we had a garden, raised and ate chickens and rabbits. So that childhood experience has always stayed with me and influenced me.

After the farm, my mother and I moved to a duplex closer to the center of town, and it was a nicer place to live. The roof didn't leak, for example. A widower lived in the nearby house with his two children, a boy and a girl. He was a machinist, and he married my mother when I was seven. His name was Rex Potter. He was legally my stepfather, but I always called him "Dad" and thought of him as my father.

We moved into his duplex, lived there a year, then we moved to a town called Rialto. It had been established by Italians, and was named after the bridge over the Grand Canal in Venice. My parents managed to buy a house in Rialto and we grew up there. My mother ended up living in that house for about fifty years.

FIFTEEN ACRES OF BOYSENBERRIES, AND A COW, AND CHICKENS, AND A PIG, AND A RABBIT.

Whose idea was it that your father would adopt you and that you would carry his name?

Mine. He didn't adopt me—they couldn't afford it. However, because my mother was a teacher, she could change the school records, so she changed my name from Rowe to Potter. That happened soon after they married. Much later, when I was twenty-six, I wanted to get a passport and had to show my birth certificate. The authorities said they could only issue a passport under the name of Rowe, because that's what was on the certificate. So, I made an appointment with a lawyer, and we went to the courthouse. There, the judge asked me, "Do you owe anybody under the name of Rowe?", "Did you commit any crimes under the name of Rowe?", and all these legal questions. I said, "No, no, no", and he said, "Well, I declare your name is Potter", and gave me a certificate. So I went back to the passport office and got my passport.

How would you describe your relationship with your mother, your father, and siblings?

The relationships were basically quite good. My mother understood me better than my father did. He was not close to me, but not distant. We didn't have a lot in common. My father was a rather conservative person in various ways—traditional, patriotic, full of slogans, sayings and platitudes. He was not an academic person but was quite intelligent. He didn't know what made me tick, but he married my mother, and he loved her, and he was a great blessing to me.

My brother, Bill, and my sister, Dee (Dolores), were two and four years older than I. We were a blessing to each other, although my brother and I playfully tormented my sister, of course. Although there were plenty of conflicts among the three of us, we were generally supportive of each other. As a family, we were not the hugging and kissing types—it was not a close affectionate relationship in that sense. We were psychologically okay.

So you grew up in Rialto?

Yes, my siblings and I went to school in Rialto, and then to junior high, and high school, and we had a lot of normal experiences. I was an active child. I played the clarinet, I was in a band, and then in high school I was the drum major. The drum major is the one who carries the big stick, walks in front of the band on the street, leads the band on the football field, and blows the whistle.

Did you have a girlfriend in high school?

Yes, I had more than one—sequentially, of course. I also had a girlfriend in college. These relationships were both close and social. There was one young woman whom I thought I might want to marry, although the relationship didn't work out. Over time, my interest in monasticism grew, and I became less focused on romantic relationships.

Were your parents both Christians while you were growing up?

We went to the First Christian Church, which at that time was in an old beautiful building that has now become the museum of the city of Rialto. My parents were very active and ran the youth group in this church.

You can't see inside a person, but as far as I know, my father was a Christian and my mother was not. My mother became a

Christian after I left home. Some colleagues of my mother's went to meetings at Campus Crusade, which had been founded in the neighboring town, and invited my mother to a Bible study. She became a Christian because of these Bible studies, after she had been working in a church as a leader and elder for many years. Becoming a Christian was a big surprise to her. She had been in the church until then because it was a place where she could have friends and be socially involved, work with the young people, and use her gifts—and because her husband wanted to be involved. Church had been a nice and positive experience, a place to take her children. Then she got saved.

Do you remember good stories from your childhood church?

Yes, I remember many good stories, but also some bad ones. There was a guy that came from the Claremont Seminary to the church in Rialto as a student youth worker. He was a liberal theologian, and I remember him teaching us about the feeding of the five thousand. He said the miracle was that the people actually had food, and Jesus motivated them to share it with each other. I was thirteen, and I remember thinking that was nonsense. He was a really good storyteller, but he didn't tell true stories. Politicians and a lot of people tell very convincing stories, but they are not necessarily true. So storytelling is a neutral gift. It can be used well, and it can be used badly.

What kind of work did your parents do?

My father, as I said, worked as a machinist, but he broke his leg badly in the machine shop and couldn't stand on the cement floor anymore. So he became a salesman. He sold restaurant supplies, and drove a car with samples over a large territory. He would get in the car early in the morning, and would drive a hundred and fifty miles during the day, visiting different restaurants and hotels. He showed his products, and always enjoyed meeting people and talking to them. He never made a lot of money, but a lot of his clients really liked him. He was well known and popular in the whole town of Rialto. When he died in the 1980s, the town newspaper's headline read: "Mr. Rialto Dies".

My father didn't make as much money as my mother did as a schoolteacher, but combined they bought a house, paid the mortgage, and we ate every day. Money was a bit tight, we weren't wealthy, but we were okay. We didn't go on fancy holidays or fly to places, or put a swimming pool in the backyard, but we were fine. My mother was a master teacher and the University of Redlands sent student teachers to her. After I left home she had some health problems. Teaching became a bit stressful, so she became a librarian. She really liked that work.

How old were you when you left home?

I was eighteen. I didn't go far. I rented a flat in the same town for several months. I was attending college in San Bernardino at the time, and eventually moved to San Bernardino and rented a small house there.

Why did you decide to move out?

I was the last child at home. There came to be tensions of lifestyle with my parents, and my mother suggested that I move. I moved walking distance, actually. My mother could walk over and see if my laundry was okay, and I ate once a week with my parents. When I moved out we became close friends. It was a good move, a good change. Sometimes my mother would call me and say, "I need to go to the mall to do some shopping." She needed me because she would always lose the car. She never remembered where she parked the car. Sometimes she had to call my father and he had to come and get her, and then they had to go back late at night to find the car, when hers was the only one in the parking lot. It was so embarrassing to her that she would call and say, "If you come to the mall with me, and remember where the car is, I'll buy your lunch!" It was a good deal for both of us. I got to see my mother and she got to find the car.

How old were you when you had your first job?
I was twelve and delivered newspapers. Shortly after that I mowed lawns. I delivered newspapers for quite a few years, and so did my brother. We used the money we earned to buy a bicycle and other things we needed as teenagers. When I was in college, I was a secretary for an insurance company. I worked every morning five days a week, and then every afternoon and evening I took courses at the college. I made enough money to pay my rent, to pay my car, and to pay the gas. The college tuition was low, as it was a state college. I had a job all through college, and looking back I can't say that I would recommend that, because I really burned out a couple of times.

What did you study at the college?
General studies, but I majored in music. I spent four years in college although never graduated. Studying music became meaningless to me.

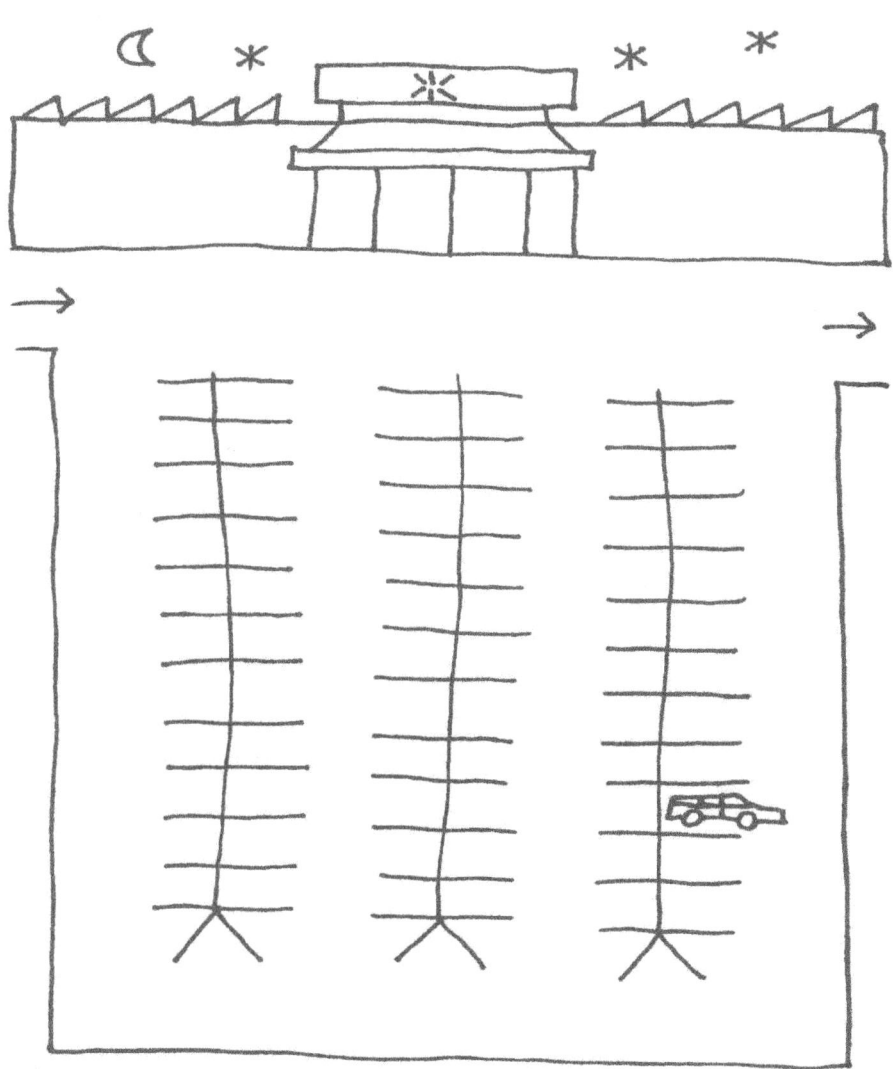

It wasn't real, there was nothing absolute about it, and I've always been interested in absolutes. After college I went with some friends into the mountains. I worked with these people in a decoupage business, and later I went into the construction business framing houses. It paid well, but it was not interesting for me. Then I met some hippies next door who had a workshop on the highway where they made candles and leather goods. We became close friends. They were into various kinds of supernatural phenomenon, and they smoked lots of dope. They also did psilocybin, Jimson weed and other really trippy psychedelic things, which for some reason I never did. I stopped the construction work because the United States post office was going to open a rural postal station in this village, and it was possible to make bids on doing it. My friends were renting a large building and I was able sublet some space from them, and eventually I became the contract postmaster for the village. People had to come to get their mail, so I saw almost everyone every day. In the morning I was a postmaster five days a week. In the afternoon I would take the mail to the main post office at Running Springs by car, then I would come back and work with my friends in the leather-and-candle business. My friends left, so I kept the post office job and took over their business. I lived in the mountains and had other friends, so I was fine. Then I moved to a bigger house, had a piano and a cat.

Other than the few years in college, did you ever get any other formal academic training?

No. My CV is blank. I have no degrees. I have no qualifications at all. I'm self-taught. What you see is what you get.

The search for truth

As a teenager what did you think about Christianity?

As I said, I was a supernaturalist, and I regarded Christianity as real and utilitarian. It was a way of coping with life. It was a way of making up for gaps in life with an emotional attachment—an emotional relationship with the supernatural reality. To me, Christianity was a useful, instrumental, utilitarian religion.

That almost sounds like Karl Marx, when he refers to religion as "the opium of the people".

I am actually largely in agreement with Karl Marx about Christianity as a religion, although I've come to realize that Christianity is not a religion. Even if you think of it that way, it isn't the only religion on the market. Religions as they are on the market can function strongly and effectively as an opiate of the people. But I no longer think that Christianity is a religion, or an opiate. "Religion" means "tying back" or reconnecting (re-ligament) with the source of reality through rituals and techniques. Christianity is the Source of reality reconnecting with us through His Word, The Incarnation and the Holy Spirit. Religion is us climbing up to God. Christianity is God coming down to us.

You were involved in churches growing up. Did you continue to be involved when you moved away from home?

When I moved away from home I didn't become estranged from my parents' church. I was a church singer, and a musician, and also got a job in an Episcopal church where I sang and acted as a choral scholar—in the English sense of a choral scholar. I thought that Christianity was true, but I asked a lot of questions, and the Christians that I knew were either not interested in my questions, or totally unable to answer them. I was convinced that my questions were valid, and that any full truth would deal with these questions.

Wasn't the Episcopalian church that hired you interested in the depth of your faith?

No. Perhaps not many Episcopalian churches in the United States would be. As far as I can remember, most of the people in this Episcopalian church were not Christians. They were Episcopalians—very churchy people. They knew each other, they liked each other, and I think there were three Christians in the whole church, which had about three hundred members. These Christians were considered to be troublemakers, and were only tolerated because they were really sweet and hardworking individuals. They talked about their faith, which some people found annoying.

Were these Christians annoyed by your questions?

No, they were not annoyed, they were only incapable of answering them, which is a step up.

So what did you do with your questions?

I began to shop around for answers in philosophical and religious groups that were available in southern California—and just about everything is available in southern California. I was in the Rosicrucian Society for some years, and then I was involved in the

Self-realization Fellowship of Paramahansa Yogananda for quite some time. The Rosicrucian Society is a combination of Christianity and Osirianism. If I remember correctly, the symbol is a cross that has a rose in the middle of it, but this faith also has strong Egyptological elements in it. Their international headquarters was in San Jose, California. They gave lessons that they would send by mail, which were nicely done. I never went to meetings, but I carefully did all the lessons, and corresponded with these people, and came to understand what they were doing. It was part of my search for truth and reality. I never really committed myself to Rosicrucianism, but I was a corresponding student for at least two years.

The Self-realization Fellowship of Paramahansa Yogananda was basically a Hindu organization. Paramahansa Yogananda came from India with the teaching of his guru, and started a fellowship in Los Angeles. He was a powerful personality, and very popular. Thousands of people came to him. He wrote a book called *Autobiography of a Yogi*, which sold millions of copies. It was a highly influential book.

What attracted you to these organizations?

They were ways of exploring reality and truth. At that stage of my life, during the hippie-drug era in America, people were searching for truth with a belief and an assumption that there was more to reality and life than a car in every garage and a chicken in every pot. People were questioning the cycle of the American dream of, "You should work hard to get a college degree so you can have a job, and earn money to send your children to college, so they can work hard..." A lot of people were dissatisfied with that, and they asked a lot of questions. The Bible-believing churches were fairly inward looking and not able to deal with these questions, or with the sociological phenomena that happened outside of the church culture. Their only reaction was to urge people to repent. There was no discussion, and the churches had rigid subcultures at that time. You were not allowed to go into church wearing jeans—it was considered dishonoring to God. You had to wear nicer trousers. You couldn't wear sandals to church—that was absolutely unthinkable. As far as I was concerned, I wasn't particularly interested in wearing sandals to church. I have a conservative streak in me, and I like continuity and I don't like change. I was happy growing up to wear conservative clothes, and to exhibit conservative behavior. I was comfortable doing that, so I never tried to identify myself through wearing flowers in my hair or anything like that. Later on, though, when I lived in the mountains, I became more of a hippie person.

Did you try to expand your consciousness like other hippies of the time?

No, I just wanted to know what is true and what is real. I didn't have a clear idea where I was going with this search, but I was fairly resolved that I would have the truth no matter what—and if the truth was darkness or death, I would have it. I didn't want to live a lie. I wanted to be genuine, and if the genuine reality was horrible, then I was not going to pretend it wasn't horrible. So I just explored many different avenues to find and to live the truth.

In your quest for truth and reality, did you get answers to your spiritual questions?

The movements I was involved in were attractive to me, especially the Self-realization Fellowship, because they had a larger view of spirituality than Christianity—mainly because they believed in reincarnation. Reincarnation is a longer-term program, a hope for perfection, where people sincerely and in a hardworking way tried to perfect their life. That was attractive to me.

Discovering Zen

How did your attention turn from the Self-realization Fellowship to Zen Buddhism?

To be clear, I was never fully or exclusively in the Self-realization Fellowship. That's not a good picture of my life at that time, because I was involved in a great number of things. I was also involved with the Bahá'i. I was like an octopus with tentacles going out in various directions searching and listening, and trying, and experimenting, and exploring. As a young teenager I had read about Zen Buddhism, and it was appealing to me. I meditated and did quite a bit of yoga while I belonged to the Self-realization Fellowship, the Episcopalian Church and the Theosophical Society. I never became a yogi—I wasn't fully committed to any of these things—but Zen Buddhism was a thread that went through all of them, and became more and more solid in my life.

Then I went to a Zen center in Los Angeles. If you go to a Zen monastery and knock on the door and you say, "Hi! I'm interested in what you're doing and I thought I would visit you", then they will likely say, "You live your life the best you can. In another incarnation maybe Zen would be right for you." But I knocked on the door, and the abbot answered and said, "Can I help you?", and I replied, "No." Then he said, "Why don't you come in?"—because he knew as a Zen Buddhist that if I knew he could not help me, then I knew something already. So I came in and he introduced me to the teacher. I learned how to do Zen meditation, called *zazen*, and started practicing more over time.

Zen has three denominations—Soto, Rinzai and Obaku. The one in Los Angeles was a Soto center. Soto is by far the largest of

the Zen Buddhist groups. The Rinzai is the middle group in size, but very hard working, and fast moving—an intense kind of Zen. There was a Rinzai Zen monastery closer to where I lived in the mountains. It was called the Mount Baldy Zen Center, and Joshu Sasaki was the master. He was the first Rinzai master to leave Japan and come to the new world, so he was a pioneer missionary. He was in his seventies at that time. Two years ago he was still alive; he was a hundred and four years old. A few years ago reports emerged that he was involved in a sex scandal, which sadly has also been true of some other religious leaders.

Do you think that the instability in your childhood in some ways contributed to your intellectual search for absolutes and interest in Zen?

It probably did. I wanted stability, but I didn't want a false stability in drugs or success or just anything. I wanted an absolute stability. That motivated me in my search, I'm sure. I went more and more often to the Zen monastery at Mount Baldy. They were always interested in absolutes, and they were the only organization I had ever been involved with that did not sell jewelry. That was important for me, because it was an indication that they were not just trying to get people's money to build a new building or something. They lived simply and they didn't have any idea of doing anything except living simply and trying to be real. In 1974 I sold everything and went and lived there. It was a disciplined lifestyle, not easy, not particularly happy, but I was satisfied that it was real—it was moving toward reality. Zen monks often travel, and go to other monasteries, and I decided I would travel too. I wanted to go to Europe, and then possibly to Japan, which is the center of Zen in the world. I had a lot of interesting experiences traveling in

America and visiting monasteries, including Catholic monasteries where zazen was practiced.

How did you sustain yourself?

I lived with a small cash flow. I had some savings, because I had sold the leather-and-candle business and the car. I lived almost without money. I went from monastery to monastery, and I was always welcome. Contemplative Catholic monasteries tend to be interested in supernatural experiences and meditational techniques, and Zen meditation is probably the fastest safe way to meditate and have supernatural experiences.

Is it actually safe?

Basically, yes. Some meditational practices get quicker results, but are unsafe—like Kundalini, which may cause mental illness. However, nothing is completely safe. For instance, it isn't completely safe to go to church because you might fall in love with a married person, or be manipulated by the leaders.

Anyhow, when I visited these monasteries as a Zen monk, the monks would say, "Come in brother, and be with us!" I was poor, and they were poor, and we had a lot in common. We were both interested in meditation. Some of the Catholic monks recommended Christianity to me, and I became interested in the Trappist lifestyle. I asked an abbot, "Can I become a Trappist without becoming a Catholic?" He said no, and I thought, "That's too bad." I've never wanted to be Catholic. But I was really interested in being a Trappist. It was so similar to the Zen lifestyle—simple and regular. It was a real community, so it was attractive to me.

What sort of spiritual experiences did you have as a Zen Buddhist?

As a teenager I was experimenting with Hinduism and Zen, when I had a strange experience. This was years before I became a Zen monk. It happened in the summer one day, when I was going to take a nap on the upper part of a bunk bed. I got onto the bed, and I lay down, and as my head touched the pillow I experienced expanding instantly to the same size as the entire universe. It was an intense experience. I don't know how long it lasted, maybe about twenty minutes. It was a sort of enlightenment experience, possibly a type of psychotic experience. It gave me hope that there is truth, there are absolutes, and you can really connect with reality as a whole.

I also had some interesting experiences in the monastery. We meditated a lot, and in-between we would see the teacher. You wait in a room, and the person who is next kneels in front of a rather heavy brass bell. When you hear a little bell in the distance, it means the student before you has gone and the teacher is ready for you. You pick up a mallet, hit this bell twice, and then you go in. I was sitting on the bench with the others. There was a big bush outside the window, and a bird in the bush was singing. Suddenly I experienced being that bird, and I was singing. It was an absolute identity experience for me. I was in the tree, I was on the bench, the bird was on the bench, and I was singing. It was an intense experience of unity. When I went to see the teacher, I did the customary bows to the ground, and then I realized that he was asleep. He was quite a dramatist, and so he was actually only pretending to be asleep. Then he woke up, and he looked out the window at this bush, and he whistled just like that bird. He looked at me, shook his head, and rang the bell. In other words, he dismissed me.

What did that mean?
It meant that my experience of the bird was not a real Zen experience. The striking thing is that he knew what I had experienced. Other students reported similar experiences.

How do you explain these things as a Christian?
In part, I don't. I don't know how things work, but I think that some people have various gifts and sensitivities and types of awareness that other people don't have. Some of these things can be developed. The Bible speaks of witches who had a connection with non-space-time reality, and who were able to interface with this reality at will, because they had developed a certain sensitivity, although it was forbidden. Because it was forbidden, I assume the Bible accepts that it's real—meaning the witch of Endor really was able to do these things. How? I'm not sure anyone has a clear picture of that. There usually is an element of magic, or shamanism in the sense of controlling or trying to control the supernatural. I think that God forbids us to use these gifts and powers, because we would feel independent of Him, and believe we didn't need Him. If we don't know that we need God, there is no realistic hope for truth or life.

Knowing that we need God is essential. Jesus went up on the mountain like Moses. Moses received the law from God, but Jesus is God, so He just gave the law in the Sermon on the Mount. The Sermon on the Mount is the manifesto of the Kingdom of God.

The first point of the manifesto is poverty of spirit. It seems to me the whole rest of the sermon is built on that point—that is, if you have poverty of spirit, the Kingdom of Heaven is yours, and if you don't have poverty of spirit, your situation is hopeless. You're lost. If you practice witchcraft or magic, you develop control over reality in ways that move you in the direction of being independent of God, or rich in spirit. By the way, some advancements in medical and scientific technology, while bringing many benefits, are also similarly dangerous. If you have trust or confidence in your own power and ability to control reality, the Kingdom of Heaven is not yours.

As you were describing your life as a Zen Buddhist monk, you mentioned that you were not particularly happy. Can you expand on that?

Yes. A Zen Buddhist doesn't have the goal of happiness, but reality. Happiness is not the point. It's much overrated. Happiness is an attachment. You can never be enlightened if you're attached to happiness. The life in the monastery was hard, and in some ways lonely, and it wasn't a particularly happy life. I didn't feel a real belonging in this community where I was, and I went looking for other communities that might be the right place for me to continue the program of my life. So I visited a lot of communities, always with that in mind—with the thought, "Maybe this would be the place where I should be."

Many people, when they find a faith, become somewhat zealous and evangelistic about it. Did you have a desire to share Zen Buddhism with others?

No, I did not. I wasn't ashamed of Zen Buddhism, but Zen Buddhists are not very evangelistic. They give people space to live their own life. However, if someone asks them about Zen Buddhism, they don't refuse to reply or to teach. While traveling, I meditated a lot, and in youth hostels and on trains I would meet people who asked me to teach them to meditate, and I did. I taught people a little bit about both meditation and yoga, as there was great interest in these practices. My behavior was somehow uncommon; it was very deliberate and calm, and therefore seen as special. People wanted to know about it. A lot of people are searching for truth, for reality, for genuineness, and they saw in me that I too was searching—and that I was really quite serious about it.

You said that you had considered going to Japan, the center of Zen Buddhism. Did you get to Japan?

No. In 1975 I bought a *See America* pass with the Greyhound bus line. As 1976 would be the bicentenary of the United States, some bus companies were offering attractive *See America* passes for the celebration. So I bought a bus pass and I went to various monasteries, visited people, and finally ended up in New York, where I stayed in my brother's flat. I got ptomaine poisoning from a pastry that I ate, and I got so sick I thought I would die. The next day, I went to the airport to catch a flight I had booked to fly to Europe through Reykjavik, Iceland. My travel agent had made a mistake and I missed the plane. I went back the next day for the same flight, got on the plane, and there encountered an old friend of mine. He was a tenor in the choir I had conducted in the Episcopal church, and he was a Christian. He had heard of L'Abri Fellowship in Switzerland and told me about it. We were astonished to see each other on this plane, and of course if my travel agent hadn't made that mistake, I would not have run into my friend. We landed in Iceland, and we were there together in the youth hostel for two or three days, and then he decided to get a job with a fishing boat and to stay there longer. I left and went on to Luxembourg. I was in Luxembourg for a few days, stayed in a youth hostel, and on the third day as I was walking down the hall, there he was again. He didn't like the fishing boat life. We decided to travel together.

He didn't have any particular plans, but I had a list of Trappist monasteries that I got from the prior of Saint Joseph's Abbey in Spencer, Massachusetts, with an introductory letter in French, German, and English, recommending me as a genuine person to be welcomed. So I had a free ticket into about a hundred monasteries in different countries in Europe, where I could just show up and stay. I wasn't just a tourist visiting, I was a monk, and I wanted to visit as a monk. I was interested to know if they did zazen or yoga. I wanted to know about their practices, to live with them, and so on. Everywhere we went we were welcomed. As I walked in the hall of a monastery, someone would come next to me and whisper, "Zazen in the chapter room at four a.m.", or something like that. It was not widely known, but in fact many monks experimented with zazen. So I would show up in the chapter room, and there would be the abbot, the prior, the novice-master, the guest-master, but no junior monks. Just the senior people. Maybe half a dozen, out of a community of fifty people.

Do you think they were Christians?

I am not the Holy Spirit so I don't have total clarity on this question. The Trappist monks were not all uniform. They probably had varying relationships with the Holy Spirit. The Trappist life is a highly ordered life, but you do not really know what goes on in a monk's heart. Thomas Merton was a Trappist monk in Kentucky, and he was basically a Zen Buddhist. He was a close associate of D.T. Suzuki, the guy who wrote *Zen and Japanese Culture*, the definitive book on this topic. Merton himself wrote *Zen and the Birds of Appetite* and *Contemplative Prayer*. He wrote a lot of books and was popular at the time when Suzuki was also popular. People are still interested in Thomas Merton. I went to visit the monastery where he lived, which was the largest Trappist monastery in the world at that time. It was a big establishment with hermitages in the forest and large buildings. One day I was walking down the main corridor, and an old man in his eighties with a long beard was walking along and saw me. He said, "Hello, I'm David", and I said, "My name is Ellis", and then he began to dance in circles around me. He asked me, "Do you know why I am like this?", and I said, "No", and he said, "It's the Holy Spirit. I have to go. Bye!" and he went on down the corridor. He was a nice man, and I thought he was genuine. I liked him. He was the retired abbot of the monastery. This is an example of Trappists not being all the same.

Did anyone try to convert you?

No. They were welcoming, and kind, and encouraging. Monasteries are not churches. They do not recruit in an evangelistic way, but wait for someone to have a monastic vocation and come to them.

Why was there such an interest in meditation among Catholic monks?

Well, they have been meditating since the sixth century, since Saint Benedict. As a result, they are interested in other people who meditate. There is less in common between a Trappist monk and a Catholic layman who works in the IT business, than between a Trappist monk and a Buddhist monk. The Trappist and Buddhist monks both live in community, wear special clothing, and are under vows of obedience and poverty. They both meditate, and they do religious practices several times a day. Their lives are very similar.

Becoming a Christian

After visiting all the monasteries, did you go to L'Abri?

My old friend—the one I encountered on the plane to Europe—wanted to visit L'Abri, and I went with him. There was only one problem: he did not know where it was. He only knew it was somewhere in Switzerland. I asked him what L'Abri was, and he said it was a community of Christians who think. I was skeptical about this. But since he had gone with me to several places, I decided I would go with him. We were going to hitchhike to Switzerland from Mainz, Germany, and one of the first cars stopped for us on the motorway. A young man from Neuchâtel, Switzerland, picked us up in a little *deux chevaux* car. He invited us to his flat and took us out to a meeting with his friends. We went into a big barn up in the mountains, and into what felt like a meeting of witches. There was a guy with a bowie knife—it's the only bowie knife I've ever seen in Europe—and he was throwing the knife into the wooden table, and then picking it out, and then throwing it again as he was sitting in a captain's chair. After a while, he put his hands on the arms of the chair, lifted his body up, turned himself upside down, and walked back and forth across the ceiling standing with his hands on the arms of his chair. He was immensely strong, like an acrobat. My friend and I looked at each other, and we thought we were going to be eaten. We excused ourselves and left. We had no idea what we were going to do. We walked out into the snow with no transportation, but we somehow knew we needed to go away from this place. Our host followed us out and took us to his place for the night. In the morning, he offered to drive us wherever we wanted to go. He did not know where L'Abri was, but managed to find it. He was not a Christian, but he served us like an angel. It was Thanksgiving Day 1975. A big turkey dinner had been prepared at L'Abri, and we were invited to join the meal.

Were you not a vegetarian at the time?

I was, so I didn't eat the turkey, I just ate the vegetables. Everybody was talking and it was noisy, and there were children. I thought it was a crazy place. My experience of spirituality was one of silence, and L'Abri was radically different. There was a young woman sitting across from me next to her husband, and I leaned across the table, and said, "What is your name?" She replied, "Fearfully and wonderfully made." I looked at my friend, and he looked at me. By the way, I still know that woman and her husband—ever since 1975. I suppose this is not what she tells everybody, but somehow she felt moved to say it to me. I stayed for three weeks and then I went to Italy, because I was not convinced that L'Abri had the truth. I thought some of their ideas were dangerous, particularly the idea that there is God and not-God. It seemed divisive and not unifying.

I was in Italy for four months, traveling around and visiting monasteries. I stayed in Rome for six weeks and studied the Japanese tea ceremony with Michiko Nojiri, who was the first woman tea master to leave Japan. I have always liked the tea ceremony, because it is a magnificent art form that includes a variety of peripheral forms like calligraphy, ikebana, architecture, psychology, and even politics. It's a great, inclusive art form. While in Rome,

HE WAS NOT A CHRISTIAN OR ANYTHING LIKE THAT, BUT HE SERVED US LIKE AN ANGEL.

I went to Michiko Nojiri's zendo every day. They meditated in the zendo, where they had a keisaku, which is the long stick that the jikijitsu hits people with during Zen meditation, but no one knew how to use it. They asked me, "Can you use this keisaku?", and I said, "Yes", and they said, "Oh, please!" So I went around in the zendo and I beat them when they needed it.

When do people need to be beaten?

It's a deep and complicated Zen thing. When you meditate, you have to sit absolutely still. There are tendencies to get muscle cramps, and tendencies to fall asleep, and tendencies to become quite disoriented. The jikijitsu goes around silently with the stick, and if he sees that you are not sitting right, then he stops in front of you and he taps your shoulder. Then you bow, and he bows, and he strikes you twice on the back. It makes a very loud noise and wakes everybody up. If he does it properly, all the muscles in your back unravel, and combined with the noise it is helpful and stimulating. If you get disoriented, he will tap you and then hold the stick vertically so that you can orient yourself to it. An expert jikijitsu will also strike you if you're meditating really well, because it can boost you into another level of Zen consciousness. You cannot just go around beating people, because if you do it in the wrong moment, it can be discouraging, which is unhelpful. I carried the stick in monasteries in Europe, and I recall there was a dentist among the students who needed to be hit more than anybody. He was grateful, and later when I had a problem with my teeth, I just called him up and got right in—and he did not take any money for the treatment.

Wonderful!

Yes, it's a whole community of interesting people. I don't know exactly how to describe it.

So, you were in Rome…?

Then I went to Naples, and then to a Camaldolese monastery. It's an order that was started by St. Romuald. The monks are hermits, and I stayed at a hermitage, and then went back to Rome. I wanted to visit Assisi, and took a train there. In one compartment a bunch of soldiers were singing songs; in another were families with children, and in another were seven nuns all in black. I was dressed something like them, in my black Zen robes with a white collar. They invited me in, so I went in and sat down. Their mother superior spoke English. She asked about me, and I told her I was a Zen monk on my way to Assisi. Then she told me, "If you're ever in Rome, and you would like to meet the pope, come to my office and I will organize it." So, when I was in Rome again, I went to her office and she gave me passes to the Wednesday general audience. On Wednesday I showed up, and went into the audience hall of Peter and Paul, where there were three thousand people, all standing. There was a master of ceremonies explaining how the audience would go, and he said, "They're bringing his Holiness on a portable throne. His Holiness is in good health, and he can walk, but we carry him, so you'll all see him." Then a Swiss Guard hit the door with the butt of his spear three times. It was a huge door and it sounded like a drum. It was really dramatic. Then these vast doors opened and there he was—Paul VI in golden robes, with a miter on his head, and robes hanging down, and six guys carrying him. It was theater. The three thousand people broke into wild cheers, shouting, laughing and jumping. They carried him down the central aisle. As he went, he touched everyone he could. Someone held up a baby, and he stopped the throne, took the baby, and threw him in the air and caught him. The gesture seemed to say, "Celebrate life!" The place just exploded like at a soccer match. I thought, "This guy knows what he's doing. They've been doing this for two thousand years." He gave a little message of greeting in six languages. His English was flawless, and his French was very good, and he said, "I'm so glad you've come, it's lovely to be with you." It was like we were in his living room, and he was the host. He was absolutely relaxed. Then different groups were allowed to greet his Holiness in a special ceremonial greeting that they had prepared, and he was delighted. It in no way made me want to be Catholic, but it was a great experience.

So this did not convert you to Christianity?

It didn't convert me to Catholicism. I have a lot of friends who are Catholics, and I believe that they are Christians. They pray with me, I work with them, and we have good fellowship, but I'm not attracted to the Catholic Church as an institution. If you want to become a Christian in the Catholic way of becoming a Christian, you become a Christian through the church. I never acknowledged the church as having the power to give me salvation. I could never relate to becoming real through the church. Millions of people believe the church saves them. I can understand the motivation, but it was never convincing to me. I have read Benedict the XVI's three-volume book about Jesus, and I'm constantly recommending it.

because it is great. It's a wonderful book. I know a lot of Protestants are opposed to the Catholic Church and think the Pope is the antichrist. I have never had that kind of attitude, but I'm not attracted to give my life to the Catholic Church, and never was.

After seeing the Pope, I went to Reggio Calabria, because I wanted to go to Sicily. On the crowded train, I was alone in a compartment with a man about sixty and his wife. He spoke a little English, and I spoke a little Italian, and we talked about everything. His wife said nothing. We shared our lunch together, and I mentioned I was a musician. He said, "Il Lirico!", and began to talk about Verdi, and the opera, and all of a sudden he began to sing. He stood up, and he sang the whole of *Rigoletto*—all the voices. He knelt on the floor, and he stood up on the bench, went outside into the corridor, and put his jacket over his head and sang, "Vendetta, vendetta..." It was a wonderful, crazy performance. He wanted to invite me to his house, but it was not possible, as they were having a funeral. Then he said, "You know, my wife is the president of the Italian Association of Child Psychiatrists, and you can stay at her offices. Here are the keys. Just leave them in the mailbox when you go." So I stayed three nights in this place. Then I took the boat across to Messina.

I went from Sicily to Malta. I was there for some days, and loved it very much, and then I returned to Switzerland, to L'Abri, because I was tired of trying to speak Italian. I knew my friend was still at L'Abri, and I wanted to see him. I thought that the ideas at L'Abri were dangerously wrong, and that someone needed to help those people.

He knelt on the floor, and he stood up on the bench, and he went outside into the corridor, and put his jacket over his head and sang "Vendetta, vendetta", and came in... It was wonderful... a wonderful, crazy performance.

Isn't that the zeal of an evangelist?

Yes, I was a missionary to Francis Schaeffer. But I was a terrible missionary, because I was the one who got converted, not him.

Did this happen in 1976?

Yes, in springtime. I told them that I wanted to stay there because of my friend. They said, "You can be a student, but to be a student, we would like you to say that it is possible that Christianity is true." I said yes, because I didn't exactly understand what they meant by Christianity, and the idea of God was very familiar to me. But as a Zen Buddhist I didn't believe that God was absolute. I believed in God, but my question was, "What is behind God? What is the context of God?"

So I became a student, and I studied for about three months, mainly Francis Schaeffer's lectures on the book of Romans. I had lots of conversations, discussions, and then one evening I was upstairs in the chalet where I lived. I was reading *Escape from Reason* and I remember looking up from the book, and the whole universe changed focus. Not shape, but focus. It just shifted slightly. It was not particularly connected with what I was reading. I literally looked up from the book, and this shift took place. It was like getting different contact lenses. I saw reality as fundamentally personal. So when I looked at the Alps, I saw that they had been created by a personal Creator, and they looked slightly different.

Before this happened, other people had to work hard with my questions. I was asking questions like, "Is the non-personal necessarily sub-personal?" and "Couldn't there be a super-personal non-personal from which personality proceeds?" One way that God worked in my life was to play a sound loop in my head. When I was in college, I sang in the opera *The Mikado* by Gilbert and Sullivan, and one of my lines was: "Who are you who ask this question?" This line began to play almost continuously in my head at L'Abri, and I realized I should take the question seriously. So I asked myself, "Who is asking these questions?" After a while, I realized that the Buddhist answer is: "Asking is." But the Christian answer is: "I am asking." The "I" who is in Christ is eternal. That pinpointed the difference, and I began to realize that I had no memory of myself that did not involve asking questions. I began to see that the Christian salvation was more comprehensive, because it saved my questions. That began to move me toward Christianity.

Would you say that that moment when you looked up from the book was the moment of your conversion?

Yes. There was a woman in the room who was not a Christian. Her name was Holly. I turned and I said, "Holly", and she said, "Yes." I said, "I believe it." She said, "I am very happy for you!" Later, she also became a Christian, but as a non-Christian she said "I am very happy for you" because somehow she could realize I had arrived at something, and made a decision.

You said that you had sort of an enlightenment experience during meditation. Can a Christian experience something similar?

I think some do. I did. My conversion experience was something of an enlightenment experience.

But it wasn't like being one with the universe, I assume?

No, it wasn't like that, but it was a definite experience, like a refocusing. It was quiet, but definite, and permanent.

How did Francis Schaeffer help to facilitate your coming to Christ?

He was kind, and generous with his time, and answered my questions in public discussions at great length. Then he would ask, "Does that help?" and sometimes I would say "No", and he might say, "We need to stop now, but next Saturday we will continue with this question." And he would.

One day I was sitting in a corner, and I raised my hand. I don't know how he saw me, but he said, "Ellis!", and I said, "Dr. Schaeffer, why is God?" People started to laugh, and he shouted, "Don't laugh!" He turned to me, and he said, "I do not know. Next question." When I left the meeting, I realized I had an answer to a long-term epistemological question: "Can a human being have a relationship of knowledge with something outside of themselves that is valid?" A Buddhist would say *no*. I realized that Schaeffer knew that he did not know, and there was no way to shake that knowledge. His not knowing was not himself; he was relating to the concept of not knowing. Three weeks later I became a Christian. So, Schaeffer's answer was very helpful. It was quite ironic. Here was Dr. Schaeffer, who spent his life giving honest answers to honest questions, and yet the greatest blessing to me was when he said, "I do not know." He knew a lot, and he explained a lot, but his not-knowing was the most helpful for me.

Did you talk to other people in L'Abri about meditation? Did you meditate with others in L'Abri?

I talked with others about meditation, but I never meditated with others. It didn't seem ethical to me to be in a Christian community and working at cross purposes with that community even though I was not a Christian at that time. I said whatever I said, and some of the workers were afraid of me, and there was some stress, but I was not subversive. I did not create little clubs on the side. I felt it would be wrong, unethical, ungrateful, and bad karma to do that.

Why were some staff members afraid of you?

Because they could not answer my questions or my statements, and they didn't have very much understanding at all of my position, or my experiences, or my philosophy. It was completely strange to them. They couldn't come to grips with it.

When you became a Christian, did you immediately stop meditating in the Zen way?

I knew immediately that prayer should replace meditation in my life, but I was in a sense addicted to meditation, because it was therapeutic for me. If I had a lot of stress, or pain, or strong emotions, I would meditate; then I would be stabilized and feel better. So for at least a year after I became a Christian I did meditate sometimes, but decreasingly. I sort of weaned myself off, or God weaned me off.

The 1960s and 70s were turbulent times: the cold war, the culture war, Vietnam, etc. Did these have an impact on how you were thinking, and how you embraced reality?

I followed the news quite regularly, so I knew what was going on, but I didn't have a personal engagement with world events. Because of my Zen Buddhism I felt that I was functioning in a larger reality than these events. I felt that trying to understand them would not lead me to life and truth. So I didn't give myself to working these things out.

Did this change after your conversion?

In some ways it did. I began to think about world events and historical, political, and economic tendencies in terms of the Kingdom of God. But I don't have the kind of political mind that is capable of coming out with a solution or a counter-suggestion to save the world. I concentrate more on trying to love, to grow and to teach people some basic principles.

What happened after you got saved?
I applied to be a helper at L'Abri.

Just as soon as you were saved?

Shortly after, within a few weeks. I was accepted, and became a helper in the chalet where I was living as a student. I lived with Udo and Deborah Middelmann. Deborah is Francis Schaeffer's third daughter. They had been very helpful to me, and supportive in my becoming a Christian during my time as a student. I worked with them for almost a year. That was a learning time for me. I became more engaged in the L'Abri work, and then there was a need for someone to be temporarily the "houseparent", the person in charge of another L'Abri chalet. It was a sudden change to being responsible, but I enjoyed the challenge. Then I moved into a small chalet, and was involved in various activities like the tape-recording of lectures and sermons, and operating the bookstore. I was also involved in cooking for the students, and I enjoyed doing that.

How big was L'Abri at the time?

At that time Swiss L'Abri was quite large. There were about twenty workers and about a hundred students. A lot of people came in the seventies, as there was the great migration of young people to India searching for truth. L'Abri was on two maps. It was on the map of spiritual communities that lots of non-Christians were aware of, and it was on the map of the reformation lands. So people would go to Wittenberg, then to various famous reformation places like Geneva, and then L'Abri. It was known as a reformed community, because Francis Schaeffer was Reformed Presbyterian.

When did you first teach at L'Abri?

When I was a helper, I gave five lectures on Zen Buddhism—the history, the philosophy, the practice, the worldwide spread, and the cultural and artistic outworking and influences of Zen. I was twenty-eight years old at that time. A year after my conversion, I was invited to teach at a conference at a Bible school north of Paris. I am a musician, and this international conference was on music. The staff at L'Abri had to ask permission to accept such invitations, because someone would have to fill in for you and do your work while you were away. I think they also recognized that I was a hard worker in some ways, and was slightly overworked and stressed, and they thought that it would be good for me to have a change, so they sent me. So yes, I began teaching much sooner than is ordinary for a L'Abri person, because I had specific experiences.

My series of teaching about Zen Buddhism became part of the L'Abri library of teachings. It was important, because tutors who did not know much about Zen Buddhism could refer interested students to my lectures. It was a big project, and I took it seriously. Now, when I think of them, I'm slightly embarrassed about the lectures. They're sophomoric, too detailed in some ways, but I still hear from people who listened to them and say they were a blessing. A woman wrote me a letter several years after I gave the lectures. She was a Zen nun, and someone had given her cassette tapes of the lectures, and then she had become a Christian. So I thought if it was only for her, then the whole project was worth it.

When you were working at L'Abri, did you think that it was God's plan for your life then?

No, I did not, and still do not see God's plan for my life at all. I don't encourage people to look for God's plan for their life, because I don't think normally people see it. I think God can show it to someone, but I don't think it's necessary.

I think we're guided by the Holy Spirit more in the short-term than in the long-term. I'm guided by the Holy Spirit in my conversation with you at this point, but I'm not guided by the Holy Spirit in how I will teach and will relate to people somewhere five months from now. At that time, I hope that the Holy Spirit will be guiding me, and giving me some interesting ideas, but I will have to test those ideas to make sure that they're from Him, and not my own fantasy. This is important, because I get a lot of ideas that come through my head, and some of them work and are appropriate, and some of them don't work and are inappropriate, and I don't want to blame the Holy Spirit for all of them. Some of them are stupid.

I have this point of view largely because of working at L'Abri. L'Abri Fellowship is founded on radical principles of living by faith. If you work in L'Abri, you do not raise funds. You don't ask anybody for money. You only pray. L'Abri doesn't advertise, doesn't recruit staff, doesn't have a plan; it waits for plans to unfold. The basic work of L'Abri is to stay at home and pray that God will bring the people of His choice to you for you to serve, and to shelter, and to give hospitality, and to work with their questions and the situations of their lives. That is the basic function of L'Abri. Then there is also a going out to preach or lecture in other places, or to write a book. But that's secondary to the work. The main work is to live and to trust and to wait to see what God shows you day by day. The finances of L'Abri are deliberately precarious, so that if God would be finished with L'Abri it could close within a month or two. There is no backup. There are no savings or insurance policies that would keep L'Abri going if God were finished with it. L'Abri has no business plan at all, which does two things: it makes you really insecure, which can be healthy, because you know constantly how much you need God; and the other thing is, when the bills are paid at the end of the month, it's a miracle, and you rejoice, thanking God. However, you have no evidence that the bills will be paid at the end of the next month, so when they do get paid, it's a miracle again. You live constantly in the reality of miracle. L'Abri has functioned like that for sixty years now. Most economists would predict L'Abri's imminent demise, because "you just can't live like that".

Students need to pay a fee, though.

Yes, but these fees are approximately twenty percent of the cost. That was prayerfully established because it wasn't thought to be wise to make it free. People should pay something, and at the same time there had always been scholarships for eastern Europeans and Africans. People who came from communist countries could not pay and did not pay—there were scholarships for these people. There are still scholarships for people from Bulgaria, Romania, Belarus, and other places. If there is any extra money or any breathing space, it's given to scholarships so that people can come, who couldn't otherwise come. When I was a worker we had a salary—it was called a "gift". It was a hundred and fifty francs a month. You couldn't live for a day on that much money in the local economy.

Are there any differences between today's L'Abri and the L'Abri of forty to fifty years ago?

There are some differences in style and atmosphere, but not a lot of differences in teaching. Fifty years ago we didn't have teaching

on postmodernism, and now we do. The basic factors—living by faith, providing hospitality, giving honest answers to honest questions, and providing a shelter—have not fundamentally changed.

How did you and your wife meet?

We met in Francis Schaeffer's living room. When *How Should We Then Live?* was delivered in reel film in 1977, we needed a projector to watch it, but L'Abri did not have one. Mary had a projector, because she used it for her work in the home for handicapped children at the Chalet Bellevue, which was right next to L'Abri. So they asked if she could bring the projector and show the film in the Schaeffers' living room. After the showing of the film, I asked someone, "Who is that woman with the projector?" and they said, "That's Mary Johnson, the directress of the Bellevue Home and School for Handicapped Children." Then someone told me that she had a harpsichord. I played the block flute, which is also a baroque instrument, so a couple of weeks later I went up to her chalet and knocked on the door. She answered, and I said, "Hello, you may not remember me at all, but someone told me you have a harpsichord. I play the block flute. Would you be interested sometimes to play together?" She invited me in, showed me the harpsichord, and then we started to play together. We got to know each other, spent some time together, and then two years later, we got married. In some ways it was a difficult decision, because she was twenty years older than me, which is a little unusual. We had to think, "Lord, how would that be…", but then we decided to go ahead and do it. You have to take special care when you have that much age difference. When we were both in the working

SO I WENT UP TO HER HOUSE, TO HER CHALET WHERE SHE LIVED, AND KNOCKED ON THE DOOR. SHE ANSWERED THE DOOR, AND I SAID "HELLO, YOU MAY NOT REMEMBER ME AT ALL, BUT SOMEONE TOLD ME YOU HAVE A HARPSICHORD, AND I PLAY THE BLOCK FLUTE, AND WOULD YOU BE INTERESTED SOMETIMES TO PLAY TOGETHER?"

phase of life, there was really no difference, but when Mary retired, it was more difficult. I could not live as a retired person, but she wanted to live as a retired person. We really had to work out some hard questions.

How did you work them out?

Just day by day, by being patient. Bit by bit we just worked them out.

Is it up to us to decide who we will marry, or are people created for one another?

Predestination and free will are opposite sides of the same coin. In order for the coin to have value, we need both sides. People often struggle with the question, "Which side of the coin would you like to have?"—or, to put it another way, "Which side of the coin is true and more valuable?" I believe that this question is evil, and comes directly from the devil, from Satan. The question is an enlightenment-type scientific question, where reality is thought of as 100%, as if it can be expressed in two-dimensional mathematical bar graphs and pie charts. We try to push predestination and free will onto a flat pie chart, and then divide it up into our part and God's part. For some people, 50-50 seems somehow a logical division, but it doesn't really work because we know from Scripture that God is completely sovereign. Giving God 50% of the pie doesn't acknowledge that. We could give Him 51% and leave 49% to free will—or even give Him 99% and leave 1% to free will, but these solutions still don't satisfy. If we go even further, and give all 100% to God, then we're nothing more than chess pieces, and if we give all 100% to ourselves, then God is on holiday just watching us and doing nothing. So, again, neither of these solutions is sound. It seems to me that the best approach is to use a more Hebraic picture of reality, which is more than two-dimensional. We need to think of predestination as a plane, or disc, in which God is 100% sovereign, and we need to think of free will as another plane, in which human beings are 100% responsible. Those two planes interface and make a three-dimensional reality—a more complete reality in which God's sovereignty and human responsibility are both necessary, and in which neither can be diminished. This solution seems more satisfactory to me.

So, I chose Mary 100%, and God gave Mary to me 100%. The two functions have a relationship of complementarity, not competition. The Western mind, which is a rationalist-scientific mind, always sees these kinds of relationships as competing for space on a 100% plane. However, in a three-dimensional sphere, in which predestination and free will are in a complementary relationship, we are functioning in a 200% reality in which Calvin (predestination) and Arminius (free will) kiss each other.

Where did you live after you got married?

I moved into Mary's chalet. I was still a L'Abri worker at the time. Mary did not fully become a L'Abri worker, although we seriously considered that. She was the only person legally competent to direct the handicapped children's work, and she could not retire without closing the institution. She was involved in the L'Abri work, and we often had students come and eat in our house, but she was not a full-time L'Abri worker the way I was.

What was your main focus in the 1980s at L'Abri?

I gave a series of lectures on music history in our home. These lectures, which included musical examples, were recorded and are in the L'Abri library. I have never worked them into a book, unfortunately. I must say, I didn't do a lot of lecturing, but I tutored a lot of students, worked in the garden, ran the bookstore, and worked the technical-practical aspects of the tape library, like recording and copying and distributing the cassettes. During this time, I also began preaching and gradually did more and more of that.

How many years did you spend at Swiss L'Abri?
Sixteen, until 1991.

Life as a pastor

It must have been a major change to leave L'Abri after sixteen years to become a pastor. How was the transition?

When I became a pastor in 1991 and moved to Basel, the church paid me a salary. I think my salary was lower than any other man's in the church, which was a slight embarrassment for some people. I felt financially insecure having this salary, because I was not living by faith in the same way I had become accustomed during my time at L'Abri. In the first couple of years I went to the elders three times, and said, "Would you be willing to stop paying me a salary, and only pray for my finances?" They were business people, executives, managers, engineers, and they said, "No, we're not willing to do that." The third time I asked, they hinted that if I asked again, they would fire me. So I took the salary and adjusted to it.

At L'Abri you were guided by the Holy Spirit, but were not making plans for the future. Was it different in your church?

At the church we accepted the L'Abri idea of finances. It was in the statutes of the church that we would end every financial year at zero. If there was any money left over, it was given away, so we started at zero as an act of living by faith, which I appreciated very much. It was clearly written in the statutes of the church that the membership fee was zero. Therefore, individual people were not obliged by their membership to support the church financially. This was important so that no one would ever think that they were buying their salvation. The membership fee was zero, and at the end of every financial year we were at zero, and then we started over. As a L'Abri guy I was comfortable with that.

Why did you leave L'Abri?

I had known the church in Basel for quite a few years. I forget how we made contact with each other, but Mary and I used to go at least once a year to lecture for a retreat, or to preach, or to do something special for this church. The church appreciated L'Abri and Francis Schaeffer. This church had functioned without a pastor since its foundation, but they had grown, and they decided that it was too much for the elders to keep up with, and they were big enough to have a pastor. One of the elders and his wife came to visit us, and over supper they asked, "Wouldn't you want to come and be the pastor of our church?" I remember saying, "No, I'm working here in L'Abri. Thank you very much, but no." They said, "Well, we're looking for a pastor, and we have this list of requirements and characteristics. We'll give you the list, and since you know a lot of people, if you find someone who fits this description, put them in touch with us." They left, and I read the list. I thought, *Good luck finding this guy*. Later that night I realized that the description described me exactly, and I didn't know anyone else who fit the profile. So I began to think about it seriously. I changed my answer from no to maybe, visited the church a few times, preached, talked to them, and gave them some strong conditions. They met the conditions, and I finally said yes.

What were your conditions?

I said I wanted every morning for myself until noon for study. That included that I would not be required to go to meetings, or to answer the phone—until noon. They said, "Granted." I also said that no one should expect anything from my wife. They were hiring me, and not my wife. They said, "Granted."

Why those two conditions?

Why not? It takes time to make a sermon. I told them it takes about twenty hours to prepare a sermon, and if I work forty hours a week, half of that is sermon preparation, and the other half is meetings, visiting in the hospital, phone calls, different things. The elders agreed, but there were some people in the church, particularly women, who said it takes less time to prepare a sermon. Soon I started a preaching class, and about a dozen men attended once a month. Then a few of them started preaching, and after they preached a couple of times, their wives came to me, and said, "Twenty hours is not enough."

And your second condition, did it have to do with protecting your wife?

Yes. She was in fact quite reasonably and cheerfully engaged in the church's life, but it was entirely her initiative—things that she wanted to do, and not things that she was expected to do as the pastor's wife. It worked for her.

What were the main differences between being a L'Abri worker and being the pastor of a church?

Working in L'Abri is like working in the intensive care emergency ward of a hospital, and being a pastor is like working in a family practice. Both are good works, but it was hard to make the adjustment. In some ways I am a workaholic, and in other ways a lazy person. I am happy when I'm intensely engaged in things and multitasking. Being a pastor requires you to step back, and be less engaged and take a long-term view. When I worked at L'Abri with students, I had a short period of time to work intensely with them. A pastoral situation is not like that. You have a longer time and you have to work more slowly. It felt like I was lazy, and not doing anything, and that was hard.

How large was the church?
About a hundred and twenty to a hundred and fifty people. It was an international English-speaking church, with people from all over the world.

What did you learn as pastor of a church?
I needed to learn to delegate and to trust.

How did you do that?
When I came to the church there were elders and no deacons. That didn't strike me as biblical. At the elder's meetings, we spent almost an hour talking about money and practical things, and I thought, *This is not elders' business*. So I initiated a process and we made a new constitution of the church that prescribed deacons, and described the deacons and their responsibility. The elders were a largely self-perpetuating body. Proposals for elders came from the elders, and had to be ratified by the congregation, but proposals for deacons came from the congregation. It was like a Senate and House of Representatives kind of situation. The elders were responsible for the teaching, the prayer life and the counsel-

ing in the church, and the deacons were responsible for the financial, the social and the practical life of the church. The elders had no responsibility and no access to the money, and it was entirely inappropriate for us to talk about money at our meetings. Instead, we spent that time praying, and it was a huge improvement. The deacons really felt trusted and honored, and finally, we had a good system of checks and balances. If the deacons, who had the money, wanted to have an outreach event, they had to have approval from the elders for doctrinal soundness, or they couldn't proceed with the project, even though they had the money. If the elders had a great idea for a conference, they had to have approval from the deacons. That seemed to be quite healthy. It was healthy for me, too, because I could become less controlling. I am by nature a controlling personality, so that was helpful for me as well.

Combined, the elders and deacons were responsible for the spiritual life of the church. The people in the church had a natural and widespread tendency to say that the elders were responsible for the spiritual life and the deacons were responsible for the practical life. I was very firm in forbidding anyone to say that. They finally stopped, because they were reminded so often. I don't know how many of them really understood the basic principle that the practical is spiritual.

Like the Schaeffers before you, you are American and ended up in Switzerland, even though you could be living anywhere in the world. Can you tell me more about how you ended up remaining in Switzerland?

I don't know exactly why the Schaeffers came specifically to Switzerland, but they came to Europe on a fact-finding mission after World War II to investigate for the Presbyterian Missionary Society the condition of children and orphans after the war. Switzerland was geographically central, and was not involved in the war, so they came here and worked from here. When they founded L'Abri, they founded it here because they didn't feel that God was calling them someplace else to do it. The calling was to stay at home, pray, live by faith, and receive the people that God sends. God provided them with a chalet and permits to live in Switzerland.

I became a Christian in Switzerland at L'Abri, and I really treasured L'Abri and was thankful for L'Abri. I liked the work and the lifestyle of L'Abri, because I have monastic tendencies, and L'Abri is in some ways like a monastery. I stayed in Switzerland because I stayed at L'Abri. I couldn't stay in Switzerland for a long time without getting a permit to live here, and the Lord provided a permit for me to stay. Eventually, I got a permanent residency, so now I have retired here on a pension from the Swiss social security system, and I probably will die here. I'm an American citizen, but I've lived here since 1975. When I visit America I ask myself, *Could I live here?* The answer is always yes. That is home. I have all my childhood memories from the US. I could live there, but I don't, because I have work here. It is also more convenient to travel from here to other parts of Europe than from America. So far, God didn't give me any specific direction to go someplace else. God has given me a flat in a beautiful ancient building with good neighbors, and He gave it to me by a miracle.

How did that happen?

Mary and I were living in Basel, in the house of some friends. With these friends, I went on some missionary trips to Hungary, beginning in 1979 or 1980. Their house was a four-story house and the church where I pastored rented the flat in it for me, much below market value. We lived in that flat for seven years, but our friends' family was growing, and eventually we needed to find another place to live. I opened up a big map of Basel and saw that way in the corner there was a lot of green, and almost no buildings. There was only one large building in the green section. It was in the village of Riehen, and I put my finger on that building. I didn't know what it was, perhaps a barn, a factory, or an airplane hangar, but I said: "God, I would like to live in that building. Amen." The next day I got in the car, and drove out to look at it. The building turned out to be a *genossenschaft*, and I thought, *This is great!* So this became one of several genossenschaften I was considering in the Basel area.

What is a genossenschaft?

It refers to a corporation of people collectively owning a residential property in which they live. I have membership in the genossenschaft, and it allows me to live in this flat and to pay rent. I have put a large deposit on the flat, and if I move, I get it back.

Are you going to ever own it?

No one ever owns the individual flats. It's always owned by the genossenschaft. I had a list of twenty-three genossenschafts, and one of them was this one. I wrote a letter in English to all twenty-three of them: "Dear genossenschaft president, I'm this age, and have a wife, but no children, and we need a three-room flat. Do you have an empty flat?" Half of them answered, and most of the answers were, "We'll put you on the waiting list." But the president of this genossenschaft phoned to say, "Yes, you wrote about a flat, and next month we will have a flat available, because some people are moving." I came out here on a Saturday, and looked around, and it was fine. That was fifteen years ago. I had to meet with the executive committee. When they learned that I wanted to retire here, they relaxed. They asked, "How do you make your living?" and I—as I was no longer a pastor at the Basel church at the time—explained, "I am a missionary. I travel and I teach, and sometimes I am paid money for my teaching, and sometimes not. But there are people who believe in my work and what I do, and who send me money to support my work." They said, "Oh fine." That is the real miracle, because that is not Swiss at all. They accepted that as a normal lifestyle. I couldn't give them my employer or my salary. It was a real miracle. I thought God had obviously put me in this place, and that He would pay for it—which is a L'Abri mentality. I moved in and God has paid for it for fifteen years so far. Because of that, I feel that God gave me this flat, and He put me here, and established me here.

When my wife died three years ago, people in Lausanne where I pastor nowadays, said, "Do you want to move to Lausanne and work more for the church and be closer?" I would like that. I love Lausanne—it's my favorite city—and I speak French better than I speak German. But I think God really has to give me clear guidance to leave this flat, because He gave it to me so clearly, and I

don't have any clear indication that I should go someplace else. It's inconvenient to commute to Lausanne, but I do it, because this is my place from God.

Sometimes pastoring can be stressful. Have you ever struggled with psychological difficulties?

Sixteen years ago I was hospitalized for five weeks with severe depression. I was in a Christian psychiatric hospital. My psychiatrist who was treating my depression recommended me to this hospital after working with me for over a year, because I had gotten worse. He was a Jewish Christian Jungian psychiatrist—an interesting combination. He made me journal my dreams, and he worked with my dreams. I didn't really believe in it, I thought it was voodoo, but it was actually effective. When I told my dreams to a younger psychiatrist at the hospital, he said, "I'm not a Jungian, I'm not an expert on dreams, but I can tell you one thing. Your subconscious mind is working very hard for your health." I thought: *I think I can believe that. It is actually encouraging that I'm not against myself. I'm very, very sick, but I'm not against myself.*

How was it to be treated by a psychiatrist?

I treated him pastorally, so at the end of sessions I would say, "May I pray for you?", and he would say yes, and I would pray for him. I was really sick, but I was still a pastor. Once, I said: "We've talked about various dreams, and it's been helpful, but I haven't told you about a recurring dream that I have had since I was eight years old. I have had it once or twice a month for the last forty-five years." He said, "Would you like to tell it to me?" So I told

HE WAS A JEWISH CHRISTIAN JUNGIAN
— VERY INTERESTING COMBINATION.

him this dream, and a couple of the variations on the dream. He said, "You see, you have this dream, because of this part of your history, and this is how you are processing this thing, and this is unfinished. You haven't come to a conclusion about this aspect of your life, and the dream is working it through." He talked with me for five minutes about the dream, and I never had it again! It was spooky. In five minutes he healed me of this plague of a dream that I'd had for forty-five years! I thought he was really good at his job.

Life as a missionary

Why did you decide to stop pastoring at the church in Basel in 2001, and how did you then become an Eastern European Renewal missionary?

My wife and I started Eastern European Renewal when we were at L'Abri, so it had been going for a long time. Regarding the church in Basel, there were various difficulties. There were a lot of tensions, and eventually it was best for me to do something else. The Eastern European Renewal thing had always been there, and I had never fully stopped doing it, so I just intensified it. I had always worked a little with Youth With A Mission, and Campus Crusade and Intervarsity, and I began to do that more. I became more available to accept invitations to go places for teaching. In some European countries, I was paid an honorarium for my teaching, and in others not. For two years I was officially unemployed. Then, when the unemployment benefits stopped, there was enough other paying work, so it worked out well.

Is there a mission statement for Eastern European Renewal?
No, not particularly.

Has the focus remained the same since the founding of it?
Yes. The end of the communist empire made a lot of changes in Eastern Europe, and it made my work less subversive and underground, but it didn't change the content of what I'm teaching. It changed in some ways the capacity of people to receive the content. Christian audiences under communism were entrenched and had circled the wagons, and were desperate to protect themselves.

The possibility of freely entertaining ideas and mixing and matching and discussing was quite limited, because of fear and oppression, and that has changed.

What are the benefits of being an independent missionary versus going under the umbrella of a mission agency?

I am able to make my own decisions, and to follow the Lord's leading as an individual.

You wouldn't have that freedom working under an agency?

I don't think so. I would have to fit the parameters of an organization; I would have much, much more accountability than I have now. My program and my activities would have to be set down in advance and approved. By being completely independent I'm more flexible. And I don't have a party line that I need to maintain.

By "party line" do you mean a denomination?

A denomination, or a missionary organization's basic stands and procedure. I don't have to follow a basic procedure. I can shoot from the hip and be flexible as I go from place to place.

What was it like to visit communist countries in the 1980s?

I had many interesting experiences. My wife and I went mostly to Poland. We carried with us things that were not welcomed by the communist government, like microfilms of Schaeffer films, and books, and VHS copies of *How Should We Then Live?* that were translated into Polish. Our family doctor was Catholic. He wasn't

Polish, he was German, but Poland is a very Catholic country. Our doctor was sympathetic to the Polish situation. He knew that we were often going to Poland, so he got from various pharmaceutical companies samples of useful medications that were not available in Poland at the time—antibiotics, suppository aspirin for infants (then unknown there), and other really valuable and expensive things. I prepared a paper shopping bag that I took on the plane. At the bottom of the bag, I put illegal things to smuggle in. On the top half of the bag I put antibiotics and children's medication. When we came to the border guards—they were people who had children—they saw these things and waved us through. We never had any trouble, because we were bringing in really valuable items, which were distributed by pastors and church organizations to people who desperately needed them. We are taught to be "gentle as doves and wise as serpents", which would be a fitting description of our approach.

I was followed everywhere. Reports were made on what I did and who I met. I remember coming to an evening meeting in a church in Warsaw. It was time to start the meeting, and the pastor came to me and said, "We can't start the meeting because the police spy is not here yet. We need to wait until he comes, because then there will be a report afterwards that nothing bad happened at the meeting. If there is no report, then they will investigate it. So, we need to wait for the spy. Everyone knows who he is." For an American, this was a whole new way of living. To think you have to wait for a spy! It was quite educational to be in a different culture, where you have to work with a rather oppressive government. I remember when General Jaruzelski declared martial law, which in my opinion saved Poland from a Soviet invasion and from utter destruction. Under martial law, the news was read by an army sergeant in uniform on television. The news was not really very newsy, it was just propaganda. I happened to be with someone one night, heading to their house, and they said: "Oh, let's hurry, because at 7:30 the news comes on!" I asked, "You want to see the news?" and they said, "Yes, it's so funny!" We didn't get home in time, but as we were walking through the streets, people's windows were open and at 7:30 we began to hear laughter coming out of the windows. People had bumpers stickers on their cars saying *TV lies*.

I was very privileged to work in Poland with Marek Kotanski, who was the founder of MONAR, an organization that helped youth who were struggling with drug addiction. It was modeled after the work of Teen Challenge, which is a Pentecostal work in America that has the highest long-term recovery rate of drug addiction of any work of its kind. Marek Kotanski was not a Christian, but he became aware of the huge success of this Christian work, and he copied their methodology. I met Marek in Warsaw in the offices of the Church of Christ with the local pastor. We went into a room with a table, and we began to talk about possible things that we could do together. As we began to talk, I became very ill. My whole body ached, and I felt miserable and nauseated. I got up, and walked around the room, then I lay down on the floor. The other two guys didn't notice it; then I finally managed to sit in the chair again. We talked some more, and we made some plans, and I just felt awful. Then the meeting ended, and Marek Kotanski left, and immediately I felt fine. I thought,

This work is important, and I have to work with this man, although there is some real opposition to it. It was a strange experience, because they never commented on my odd behavior.

Did you have the same experience when you met him again?
No, I was fine after that. Then I went to the drug rehabilitation center in Krakow with my Polish translator, who is a very beautiful woman. We had just been preaching in a church, and then there was a Sunday afternoon meeting at the rehab center. I went in wearing a three-piece suit with a gold watch chain, and she was wearing a beautiful dress and her hair was nicely done, piled on the top of her head. Everyone at the center was wearing muslin, tattoos, and piercings, sitting around on dirty mattresses on the floor with their dogs. They were drug addicts. Some of them recovering, some of them not recovering, about forty people. I was supposed to speak to these people. It was not the easiest situation, so I prayed, and my translator, Eva, prayed, and our driver, a Baptist pastor, prayed throughout the meeting. We needed it. I looked at the people around me and I said, "I'm sorry that I'm not wearing the uniform." It was translated, and they did not get it. I said, "Well, you're all dressed alike, and you're all very similar to each other, and you have a culture and a society, and I am an outsider, and I don't fit in because I am a rebel." They all considered themselves rebels against the Polish culture, against the church, against communism, against everything, and they looked at me, as if thinking, "Rebel?" I said, "Yes, I come from America, and I fit in some places, and I don't fit in other places, and belonging is a very important thing. You obviously belong to each other in various ways

and I don't belong. It's a bit uncomfortable, but still I'm glad to be with you, and I hope that in some ways you will accept me. I'm not a conformist, and I'm not going to change my clothes just so that I can have contact with you." They began to look at each other, and they really started to listen. I said, "In America, if someone is addicted to heroin, we say he has a 'monkey on his back'. What do you say?" The drug addicts in Poland have a secret language, like a cockney dialect, that they use to communicate and no one understands what they are saying. They looked at each other and they asked, "Shall we tell him?" They decided they would, so they said a word in Polish. I looked at the translator, and she just burst into tears. When she recovered, she said, "It means *cringe*." That's their word for heroin addiction. Very sad. My translator was weeping because she's Polish, and they were her neighbors and they really were a mess. I said, "Actually, I would like to talk to you about a man, who was a rather radical rebel, and because of his rebellious attitude and behavior he was killed." They looked at me, and I gave a long, long pause, then I said, "His name is Jesus." Then I preached, and they heard. It was a good meeting.

Marek Kotanski, who was a professional psychologist, started a political campaign to limit the legal growing of poppies to three provinces in Poland. At the time, poppies were traditionally grown everywhere. Every housewife in Poland had poppy seeds in her own garden to use in baking. These poppies can be used to make heroin. People would go in private gardens in the night and harvest the poppies. Then they would make a drug called *kompot*. There was no standard recipe or procedure for producing the heroin; every little group had a slightly different way to do it. It was unsafe

IN POLAND POPPIES ARE TRADITIONALLY GROWN EVERYWHERE.

unsafe and impure, and sometimes it was poisonous. So, as I said, Marek Kotanski wanted the parliament to pass a law to have intensive cultivation of poppy seeds, but only in three provinces. The communist government responded (in effect) like this: *There is no drug addiction in Poland. There is no homosexuality in Poland. There is no alcoholism in Poland. We live in a worker's paradise, and we simply don't have these problems.* So Marek made big posters in the red Solidarność font. At the top of the posters, it said: *There is no drug addiction in Poland.* Just under that it said *Signed:* and the rest of the poster was blank. These were all over the cities for months, and no one signed them. No government official dared to sign them. They hung there blank, week after week, until it was obvious no one would agree with this statement. Finally, the government passed the law restricting poppy seed cultivation.

Marek drove me in his car to different drug rehabilitation centers, where people were in a kind of boot camp. They had been stripped of everything. They weren't allowed to choose their own music; they had to earn the right to choose the music they listened to. They weren't allowed to smoke cigarettes. If they smoked one cigarette they were thrown out, and if they were thrown out, sometimes they died. Their heads were shaved. They had to earn the right to grow their hair. They were reduced to nothing, and they had to build up their life in a new way. This is how it has been done in America with Teen Challenge. It works. People recover from the drug addiction, and they often stay recovered, they don't fall back into it afterwards. It's a good program. In America, unlike in Poland, rehabilitation included a lot of prayer, and prayer for healing. So Marek took me to these various rehab centers, called a meeting, introduced me, and then someone would translate for me. I would speak about salvation, healing, identity, and who we are as human beings. Then they were allowed to ask questions. Some of them were angry, and some of them were confused, so there was really strong discussion. I can remember a young woman raising her hand, sitting on the floor. She said, "You speak about God." I said, "Yes." She said, "Marek Kotanski is my god." People were nodding, and Marek was sitting right next to me. I thought, *This is an extreme situation, and from what they know so far, there is no other god, there is no other savior, but Marek Kotanski.* He was not a Christian, and this was a strong, humbling experience for me. I was completely out of my depth.

What is your most memorable lecture from those times?

I remember when I first delivered the "3 Theories" lecture, a comparison of different worldviews or philosophies. It was in Wroclaw, in 1987 or 1988. The Baptist Church was allowed to organize a lecture in the people's culture palace. They were allowed to advertise this meeting in the communist newspaper. This was the first time a Christian organization could do this. They were pretty excited and announced that a "Swiss philosopher" would lecture. While a Pentecostal pastor was driving me there, the car broke down, so we were an hour late. We arrived with greasy hands because of trying to fix the car. To our great surprise, there were hundreds of people in front of the culture palace. Loudspeakers had been put outside the building. We wanted to go into the building, but we could not because the crowd filled the hallways. I said, "What is happening? What is this event?" Someone told me that *I* was the event. I thought, *Oh no. Mercy!* They took us around to a side door and we got in. A Christian band was on stage, playing to keep the people there. The Baptist pastor was pale, because we hadn't shown up. It was a big theater with a balcony, keg lights, footlights, a stage, and a proscenium, and it was packed with people. In the crowd was the parapsychology club of Wroclaw, the witches' coven of Wroclaw, all of the paranormal and transcendental societies of the city—and, of course, all the Christians. Everybody was there: the intellectuals, the artists, the wizards in their pointed hats. It was one of the most interesting groups that I ever saw. The band came off, and I went on, accompanied by my driver/translator. Because of all the lights, all I could see was the reflection of the eyeglasses of people in the front row. The rest was black. I leaned forward and I looked around trying to see if I could orient myself, and I said: "Is anybody out there?" This was translated, and the audience began to applaud. They thought it was a deep philosophical statement. If I had said "Fish for sale" they might have also applauded. People probably thought as they cheered that they had just heard the first genuine question in public in forty years. It made me feel better. I thought, *They are on my side, we are together here, and we're going to do something together.* It had been announced that I would lecture on comparative philosophy. We were exhausted, we were stressed, so I said, "You know, comparative philosophy is as simple as one, two, three." I gave the lecture in a rather primitive form, and then there was time for questions and answers. When we came off the stage into the green room, I said, "Quick! Give me paper!"—and I took notes on the lecture that I had just given. That's basically the *3 Theories of Every-*

thing book. During the next twenty-five years I developed it, and I have delivered it hundreds of times, but that is how the lecture was first given. It seems to me that it was given to me in that stressful moment when I was out of control and exhausted.

On teaching and lecturing

You are now pastor of a church in Lausanne. How did this come about?

I had known that church while I was working in L'Abri and had friends there. I had gone to lecture at retreats and preached a few times. They have had several pastors in the last forty years. When their last pastor left, they started to slowly look for a pastor and I knew it. I knew I couldn't work fifty percent (which is what they were accustomed to), because of all my other work. I offered to work two weekends a month, which in Swiss terms is considered twenty percent. I could commit myself to that and organize my travels around it, if that would be helpful. They thought about it and prayed about it, and said, "We would like to try it." We tried it for six months, and everybody liked it. So far I've been there for nine years. I spend the rest of my time traveling for lecturing and preaching.

What is the DNA of Ellis Potter's ministry?

The center of my task as I understand it is to help people to think, and encourage them to love.

Now, in your retirement—or semi-retirement—what is your financial situation?

I have a small pension, and money from the church in Lausanne where I still work twenty percent. That's almost enough to pay for the rent, the health insurance, and the food. It's not quite enough, but other money comes from various sources. I trust God, and He makes my life work financially. Extra money comes in through honoraria for teaching, and book royalties. There are people who listen to my lectures and sermons online and are blessed, believe in what I am doing, and send me money every month or occasionally. I'm not saving money, but I'm not in debt, and I pay the rent every month. In a way, it is a kind of L'Abri financial lifestyle.

In 3 Theories of Everything, you say that "relationship precedes identity". How has this worked out in your life?

There is a default program for human life that God has given, which is marriage and children. Not everyone functions within that default program. Jesus spoke in Matthew 19 of special programs for people who are damaged or especially called. Then, at the end of that, He says, "He who can accept this teaching, should accept this teaching", which I read to mean, "If you can be married and have children, you should be married and have children, but you might not be able to for a variety of reasons." I know that some people understand this passage as prioritizing singleness. I cannot agree with that reading, although many millions of Christians do.

I have a relationship with God. I am not alone, because Jesus is with me. I speak to Him; He is with me, He keeps me, He holds me and that's good. I also need human relationships. Before I was married, I had human relationships, and then I was married for thirty-five years. When my wife, Mary, passed away three years ago, I thought I would be okay living alone, because I had previously been a monk. I enjoy being alone, and I didn't get married until I was thirty. But after a few months I realized it was not okay. I didn't do well living alone.

How did that realization come?

I became a bit depressed, a bit defused and unfocused, and undisciplined in some ways. I made efforts to reestablish my life—I redecorated the flat to some extent, I got a new dining table and a new carpet, and I changed some things, which was wise and helpful—but it was not enough. When people visited and stayed in the extra room, I did better. I am open to having visitors, and possibly a helper to live here. I am waiting for the Lord to guide and provide.

PART 2:
Reflections and Insights

On storytelling and language

Everyone who has heard you teach or sat at a table with you can confirm that you are an amazing storyteller. How did you become one?

My father liked to tell stories, and he was good at it. He told stories that were jokes mostly, and I like to tell jokes, and I tell them well, with drama. I remember telling stories when I was a child. It was the thing my father enjoyed most about me. We would be some place visiting, and he would say, "Ellis, tell the story about your gym coach" or something. He was proud that I could tell a story.

Did you have to work on that gift?

Most gifts involve work. I script text in my head for sermons, conversations, and storytelling. In that sense I work at it, but in another sense, the phrases, timing, sequencing, and drama just come. Often the script is visible in my head and I can read it like a banner that goes across a screen. In a way, I read the story to you. It's a river that flows, and carries the people with it.

My American missionary friends like to say that you can always take an American out of America, but you can never take America out of an American. Do you have that experience about yourself?

Actually, I don't. Most Europeans don't think I'm an American until I tell them. They mostly think I'm English, because if I speak French or German, I speak with an accent. When they speak English to me, they think I'm English, because I learned English as a second language. My mother tongue is American. I can still speak

IT'S A RIVER THAT FLOWS, AND CARRIES THE PEOPLE WITH IT.

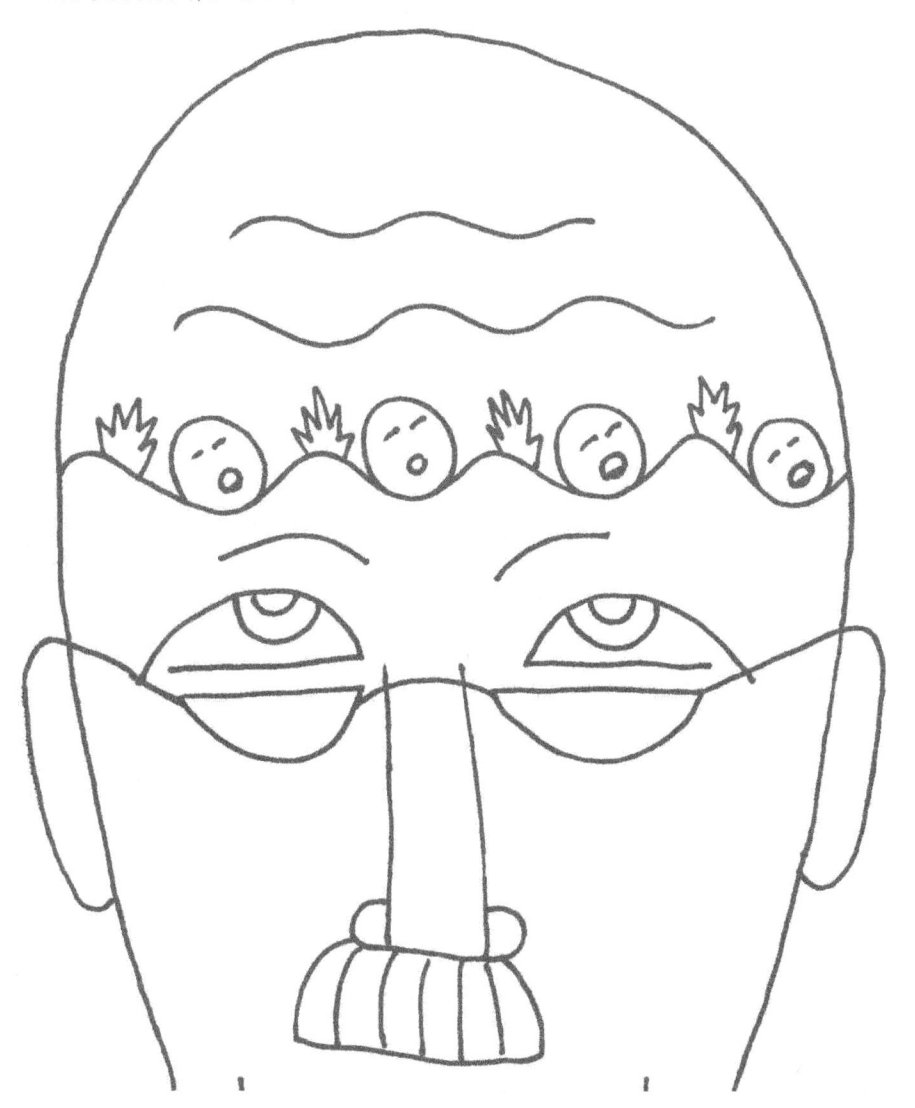

American fluently, but with an accent, and when I go to America people ask me where I am from.

I learned English because I found that if I teach in English I'm better understood, and the translators have an easier time. I have visited England many times and learned English phraseology. A great triumph happened three years ago, when I was in the south of England and someone from the very southern coast was talking to me. As we spoke for maybe ten minutes, I was really trying to speak English, and he said to me, "Are you from Leeds?" I remember thinking, *Yes! He thinks I'm English! He knows I'm not from here, but he thinks I have some strange northern accent.* That only happened once, but I took it as a confirmation.

What other languages do you speak?

I speak bad French, bad German, and bad Italian, and a few words of Polish and Hungarian. I can also smile in Korean.

On prayer, meditation and making decisions

What is the difference between prayer and meditation?

Prayer is a relationship—it is the verbal part of a relationship—and it belongs with other parts of relationship like work and obedience. Prayer integrates and coordinates with other aspects of life. Meditation is more a thing in itself. It's more directly and specifically therapeutic. This is why transcendental meditation, or TM, was so popular. It is specifically therapeutic. It reduces your stress and helps you to concentrate. It's almost like a specific medication that only treats certain aspects or symptoms of the fallenness of the person. Prayer is more generally integrated with various other parts of our fallen nature, where we are broken and confused, and need redemption and healing. The effect of prayer is not so specific and clear as the effect of meditation. Prayer is better, because it's integrated in the whole of life. Prayer maintains relationships. Meditation eliminates relationships. Prayer is more real than meditation, because relationships are fundamental to the reality in which we live.

Would you ever encourage Christians to meditate?

There are different forms of meditation. An Asian or Monistic (as in *Monism*) form of meditation precludes thought, so in order to meditate you have to stop thinking. The Bible also speaks about meditation. Words such as "meditation", "prayer", and "thinking" appear in the Bible, and don't mean exactly the same thing. Biblical meditation is not linear or rational thought; it is another form of cognition. Nor is it speech (which is what prayer is). It is not thought with an agenda or rational purpose. It seems to me that biblical meditation—as I have learned from Psalm 119—is about God (for example, "I meditate on your precepts", "wonders", "laws", or "statutes"). We can meditate on different aspects of God, as if those aspects or concepts are hovering over the net or web of our mind. All meditation begins with words. Monistic meditation moves away from words. Biblical meditation retains the words. The biblical words stimulate our non-verbal awareness of a concept (such as God's "mighty power", or whatever aspect of God we are meditating on). This way we give passive space for the Holy Spirit to connect these concepts to the web of our mind. When that connection is made, we begin to think and pray in a way that is illuminated by the Holy Spirit. So in my understanding, Christian meditation cannot be separated from thought and prayer, but helps with thought and prayer. Within this general "method", everyone finds their own way of relating to God. God relates to each of us uniquely.

Can there be listening phases in a prayer?

The Bible teaches about "waiting" on the Lord, and being still before Him. This is a receptiveness to God's engagement and illumination. Some Christians expect to "hear God's voice". It seems to me that the people in the biblical accounts, who heard God's voice, were not listening for it, but were always surprised by it. So, I believe that God speaks to individual people, and I believe that people sometimes hear God's voice, but I'm not sure that listening for it has much to do with it.

We should be careful about teaching people to "listen" for God's voice, because sometimes people fake it, lie, make it up, feel guilty, or pretend. Negative results can develop. Sometimes people feel second class, like the people who have never spoken in tongues in certain charismatic churches. Some think that if you don't speak in tongues, you're a second-class Christian, or if you don't hear God's voice, you're a second-class Christian. I know people who have pretended to speak in tongues, and I know people who have pretended to hear God's voice. We have to protect people from this kind of thing.

That doesn't mean God cannot speak to us. Last May when I turned sixty-seven, I began to have vague thoughts about a different lifestyle. I was thinking maybe I should stay home more, write more, counsel more by Skype, and concentrate on other parts of my ministry. It was nothing definite, just a vague thought. A few days later I was asleep in the night, dreaming of this and that, and suddenly I heard a quiet, calm, masculine, high-pitched clear voice, which said: "You have a good mind. Travel the world, and help people to think." I woke up, I sat up, and I said, "Okay." I didn't know what else to say. I'm convinced it was God speaking to me, and it wasn't exactly the message I was looking for. I was vaguely looking in a different direction, and I was not listening, but I heard. It only happened once.

How do you make important decisions?

In a variety of ways. In the Book of Acts, when people make decisions, we read, "The Holy Spirit told us", or "It seemed right to us", or "We decided". All these suggest different ways of making decisions. I think it's important that Christians realize this—

there is no standard method of getting God's blueprint for making decisions. One decision isn't going to be made the same way as another decision is made. Sometimes I get a strong sense, but sometimes I don't have any sense or any feeling, but the decision still has to be made. I find a reasonable idea, and bring it to God. It is almost like saying: "God, I thought this through, and I'm going to do this, and if it's not right, stop me."

You are an intellectual, yet also experiential and intuitive. How do you reconcile these different aspects of life?

I would say they are reconciled in love. When I preach, the sermons are not unintellectual. I try to guide people through a thought process of understanding, but the message is always: *God is love and the reality of life is love.* You can have an intellectual understanding of many things without love, but it doesn't bring life.

THERE IS NO STANDARD METHOD OF GETTING GOD'S BLUEPRINT FOR MAKING DECISIONS.

On culture

In what ways were your mission trips formative?

I have learned to understand a wider variety of different cultures, which has been a painful process and a steep learning curve. Nevertheless, I'm thankful for and satisfied with the things that I've learned about being with different kinds of people and understanding how they learn. If you make a mistake about what their learning culture is, you fail as teacher. They cannot learn from you and you teach them nothing, which is a horrible experience.

Can you give me an example of how Hungarians learn?

It is a kind of a mixture. Hungarians like a good amount of schmoozing. They like to hear nice, cheerful, funny things that are not necessarily content-full, but connecting. If you do quite a bit of that, then they relax, feel at home with you, and they can concentrate on learning something. This is my experience.

You have also lectured in parts of Asia. Can you tell me about how Asian cultures learn?

In my limited experience, they tend to learn by rote. They don't learn so much by thinking things through, as by taking in data and memorizing it. When they're allowed to ask questions, at first they cannot, because they've never been allowed to. And then when they start asking questions, some of them break through to thoughtful questions, while some of them can only ask data-type questions. When given permission to truly ask thoughtful questions, some Asian students explode with enthusiasm and creativity.

If you lived in the U.S. would you teach about the same topics in a similar way that you teach in Europe and in other parts of the world?

I teach about the same topics everywhere in the world, but the way I teach changes a lot from place to place. If I were in the U.S., I might use illustrations from baseball or football, or other typically American cultural phenomena.

On faith, salvation and doubt

In your understanding, what is necessary for a person to be saved?

I think that the foundation of salvation is not being good, but knowing our need of God. I think that people do many good things, and they're not saved. So doing good wouldn't be the criterion for me. We talked earlier about the Sermon on the Mount, and that the foundation of the whole manifesto of the Kingdom of God is poverty of spirit. So if a person does good things, but has no poverty of spirit, and they don't know that they need God, they cannot have a saving relationship with Him.

What if they know they need God, but haven't heard the gospel? Let's say they believe in some sort of supreme being?

I think that God meets people who seek Him with all their heart. I believe it's promised. If they know that they need to be healed, forgiven and justified, and they long for this, then God will satisfy that longing. But the foundation of understanding must be a realization that "I don't fit", "I'm not right" and "I need to be made right", so that "I belong in reality". That would be the prerequisite for salvation.

So if that doesn't happen, there is no hope for the person?

I don't see any indication in Scripture that there is.

In 3 Theories of Everything, you state that doubt is important in our growth as Christians. Are there any things concerning your faith or your life that you have doubts about?

I have doubts about myself, but I don't think I have any doubts about God. I don't have any doubts about God giving love and salvation and healing, but I have doubts about me receiving those things. I don't have any doubts about the truth of Scripture, but I have doubts about my ability to read and apply it. Some Christians suffer from a form of perfectionism, in which they believe that they should not have any doubts, and that everything should be perfectly clear to them. Fallen but saved people in a fallen world should not expect perfection. If we don't have any doubts, it is difficult to change or grow.

How can those doubts help you in your growth?

The doubts help me to realize that I don't know everything, and need to be learning. The doubts help me not to get stuck in a frozen set of static ideas. The doubts stimulate me to ask lively questions. God's truth in Scripture is solid and dependable, but also a living truth that is not a mathematical formula. A question that I've been working with recently is whether eternity is created or not. I know that time is created. I tend towards *not*—that eternity is not created—but that's not totally clear to me.

There was something that really struck me in 3 Theories of Everything. You seemed to suggest that if Jesus' bones were found, then you would reconsider your Christian faith. Does your identity as an intellectual person come ahead of your Christian identity?

No. They are the same thing. They are integrated with other factors of my life. I wouldn't say that my emotional life, which is lively in my case, is ahead of my Christian life or identity. However, if you take away all the evidence for faith in the historical context, and the internal consistency of the Scriptures, and the eyewitnesses of the resurrection of Christ—the fact that the bones were not there—you no longer have a Christian identity. You would have a fanatical identity. You would have faith in faith, and not faith in truth. That would be a disaster.

So you cannot imagine that somebody has faith in God based on a relationship with God instead of facts, historical facts.

I cannot understand why one would separate the relationship from the facts. They belong together. They are integrated. They are complementary. You have a relationship with your wife, but you don't choose between the relationship and the facts. You have to have them all together for the full human reality of your relationship with your wife. You don't just have your emotions about your wife without any facts. That's not real. That's not life. You can't build on that, and you can't live it. They have to go together. I would say the same about a relationship with Jesus Christ. I think it is possible for a person who is isolated or illiterate to have a living relationship with Jesus Christ with very little information. There are certain dangers in that. I think God wants us to have information, and that's why we have the Bible. We shouldn't set aside the Bible and say, "First of all I have a relationship with Jesus Christ", and then decorate it and substantiate it with the Bible. I think that's a dangerous way to proceed.

For you, if Jesus' bones were found, it would mean that the Bible is not true?

Yes. If the Bible is proven to be false, the foundation is taken away. It doesn't mean that I've not had emotions about a Jesus that I believed is resurrected and alive. I did have those emotions,

I did have those experiences, but I would have to begin to think that they were caused by psychological hysteria or something else—if the evidence were not there. If I only have the evidence, the Bible, or if I only have logic, but I have no emotions of thankfulness, or sorrow for my sins, or a desire to obey and a longing to be closer to God and be more like Jesus, then my life is very poor, and I may not even be alive. If I have those things, but I don't have the evidence, I could be having faith in faith.

To be honest, I think a lot of people do have faith in their faith. I remember, I was in a discussion in a large boarding school in Chesieres, near Swiss L'Abri. The chaplain of this boarding school was a Christian. During parents' week, when all the influential and wealthy parents from around the world came, he organized a debate. There was a Jewish rabbi, an imam from Geneva, and a Presbyterian pastor. Although I was a Christian at the time, I agreed to represent Zen Buddhism, on the condition that I could say at the end of the debate that I am no longer a Zen Buddhist. The question of the debate was: "How do you know that God exists?" The imam spoke first, and he spoke at some length, and his speech was peppered with emotional religious slogans, but in essence what he said was, *I know that God exists, and if you don't agree, you will die.* Then it was the rabbi's turn, and he said: "I know that God exists, because I believe in Him so strongly that He must exist." This is total humanism. *I know, because I believe.* No evidence, no Scripture, no Torah, no history—only "my faith teaches me that God exists". A Nazi can have the same experience, and so can a communist, a Buddhist, or a Hindu. Their faith teaches them that these things are true. Christianity is not like that.

Then, as the debate went on, the Presbyterian pastor spoke. He didn't have enough time to make a really full statement, but he talked about a circle of evidence (circumference of reality): the authority of Scripture, the shape of the universe, the personal nature of the cosmos, and other good reasons why he knew God existed. At the end, he also included his own personal experience of God.

Then I spoke as a Zen Buddhist, and I said: "I do not know that God exists, and I do not know anything else." Then I stopped talking, and the applause began to rise like a tsunami. Unfortunately, I seemed to win the debate. At the end of my remarks, I said, "I am no longer a Buddhist, I have become a Christian." People objected that it was unfair that I had spoken as a Buddhist, when I wasn't a Buddhist. What was unfair? I won the debate!

The rabbi, as I mentioned, basically said that God must exist because he believes in Him so strongly. Without revelation or Scripture, or historical veracity, this is a humanistic or sentimental approach to truth. There are Christians who seem to know in this same way. I like to ask this kind of person: "Who is Jesus Christ before you were born?" Some of them don't have anything to say about Jesus, but only about their experiences of "Jesus". They only know about themselves. This is the danger of allowing our emotions to fill the whole picture and to overshadow the evidential part of our relationship with God. I realize that this sentimentalism is attractive and relaxing. It is experiential, delicious and energetic. It feels authentic, and in fact it is authentic, but I think authentic is a negative factor, because authentic comes from *"auto"*, the "self", and the only authentic part in reality is God. I am not authentic. I can be genuine, I can be honest, but I am not authentic in the sense of beginning with or from myself. I am not self-generated. In the postmodern world, self-generation or authenticity is of high value, and people are praised for it.

I think people are praised because they seem to be congruent and genuine, and they associate that with being authentic.

Yes. Authentic is often taken to mean "sincere", but it does not mean "sincere". I have a great respect for language, and I think if we twist language in this way, we will lose the power of language to shape our thinking realistically, and we will become confused. We will learn not to trust language and evidence, including the language of God. We won't take God seriously in what He says in His word; we will say "whatever" at the end of our sentences, and eventually we will not take ourselves seriously either. Then, there will be a decreasing stability in our identity in Christ and in relationships with others and the creation.

On music and art

As I look around your living room, I see a lot of instruments. There is a keyboard, there are block flutes on the wall, and there is a dulcimer.

Actually, I made that dulcimer when I was in L'Abri, but I don't play it much anymore. I used to play it at L'Abri. It makes a nice mellow, folky, Bluegrass kind of sound. I had a little photocopied group of songs that we could hand out, to sing a song with the dulcimer before we ate. I play unusual medieval Bluegrass folky, simple instruments. I don't play the guitar, but I played the ukulele for a while, although it was never a major thing in my life. I played penny whistle, but nowadays I play a lot of block flute (recorder). I recently gave a concert in Vienna and I play for weddings, too.

In my youth, I played the clarinet from the age of eight, and all through high school and college. I played the Mozart clarinet concerto with orchestra, the Brahms clarinet quintet, and the Mozart clarinet quintet. I was also the concert master of the United States College Honor Band. We flew to Michigan to work under William Revelli, to give a concert at Hill Auditorium at the University of Michigan. Playing the clarinet was a large part of my identity. I was never a brilliant clarinetist, but I really loved to play, and I did okay. I played all the right notes at the right time, but it was not great art. When I was twenty-one, I changed to block flute, and have kept playing it since then. I take lessons from a professor at the Academy of Music in Basel once a month. I have to prepare homework. I play sonatas, and he corrects me or gives suggestions for interpretation. I'm slowly getting better, and would say I'm an advanced beginner at this point.

In your youth you worked with hippies, but never took psychedelic drugs. Did you take psychedelic music?

I never played in a group, and I don't categorize my understanding of musical art according to commercial labeling, although I have noticed one interesting thing. I'm not sure if it's true anymore, but in music shops they would have a section of new age music, and a section of contemporary Christian music, and they were always right next to each other, because the music store owners knew they were basically the same thing. I realize this is a violent opinion. New age music is sometimes called meditation music, and this genre became popular at the time when contemporary Christian music also became popular. These types of music were quite similar. They were designed sonically and in terms of the relationships within the music of rhythm and harmonies and melody to be minimalistic. The "rhythm rhythm" was very slow, which means that the space between the changes of the rhythm was very long. When you make music like this, it functions in the consciousness very much like smoking marijuana. If you smoke marijuana, and then you look at a flower, or a spot on the wall, or at someone's clothing, you become intensely engaged with that and have a sensation of deep understanding and wisdom, and penetrating knowledge—which are true sensations. But the focus of the sensations is so narrow that it makes you stupid, because you are engaged with a very small part of reality and don't understand nuances and relationships in a wide spectrum. Meditation music dumbs you down in this way. It makes you stupid and moves you towards death, although it makes you feel intelligent and alive, because of your intense engagement in the narrow spectrum of reality. Christian music can do the same thing. Perhaps not so much in the last ten years, but twenty or thirty years ago.

Those are harsh words!

I know, but I'm concerned about the music that Christians use in their churches or in their homes, because it is sometimes go-to-sleep music. It's can be comfortable music, but also dumbing-down music. It's not stimulating, it doesn't make life larger, but it feels really good, so people like it and buy it. The music industry finds out what people like, and what they will pay for, and produces it.

Earlier you said that Christians are allowed to meditate on certain aspects of God. Is it possible that Christian music that "dumbs you down" might every so often help in focusing on certain aspects of Jesus?

I suppose it would be possible, but I think it's unlikely, particularly because much of Christian music is narcissistic in terms of what it says about Jesus—so much so that I like to ask students the question I mentioned earlier: "Can you tell me, who is Jesus before you were born?" Often people start to talk about "Jesus is the one who loves me", "Jesus is the one I adore", "Jesus is the one I worship". I say, "No, no, tell me about Jesus without using the words *I, me* or *mine!*" Then, often, people have nothing to say, because they don't really know anything about Jesus. They only know something about themselves, and their knowledge of Jesus is experiential, sentimental, and self-centered, which is unhealthy.

Can art be therapeutic? Can art help us get closer to God?

I lecture about art and work with artists. I have strange and highly controversial ideas about what art is. I don't know if my answer is going to belong to your categories. I think that art is "deliberate human action". Art is related to the Latin word for arm or articulation (*artis*). It means something that is made by the arm of the human. So, my definition of art is a big circle, but it leaves out everything that God does. What God does in creation is nature, and I see a big divide between nature or natural, and art or artistic. So in my understanding art can by definition never be natural. It has to be artistic, which means *artificial*. What is natural is natural, and it has its own beauty, its own value. We thank God for it and we enjoy it. But it's not art. The sunset is not art, but the photo of the sunset is art. We are closer to God when we do art, because He commands us to have dominion over the creation. The creation is natural, and human beings are commanded by God to be kings, or like gods over the creation, and to continue God's creative process of making relationships. God divided the land from the sea, the plants from the animals, the fish from the land animals—always making complementary relationships. Then, He gave to human beings the privilege and the responsibility of continuing that process of creating relationships, but also of imposing in a manipulative way their own imagination, their own concept on nature.

One of the most important ways that this is done is agriculture. For instance, wheat naturally grows along the banks of streams mixed with other plants. But human beings say, "Wheat, you will grow in this field alone." This is unnatural. Wheat would never naturally do that. The wheat field is art. It is artificial, made by the arm of the human. In order to have any kind of culture, or civilization, human beings have to function artificially. They cannot only function naturally, because the human being is the naked ape. We're vulnerable. We have no claws, we have no fur, we don't have scales, we don't have big teeth, we're not very fast runners, and we don't have tails to swing from. We're really ill-equipped naturally. The only place we can function naturally is maybe in an equatorial rainforest, where food is constantly available from the trees, or dug up in roots, or something like that. We could sleep in the trees, and then we would be natural. But we're not natural, we're spiritual, and we're artistic. We live artificially. We impose our concepts on nature to reshape it creatively and to make new kinds of relationships.

So we grow wheat in fields, and then we harvest it, we store it, we keep the rats out of it, and we make beer out of it—which the rats won't eat. And we make bread with beer, which we can keep through winter without it molding or the rats eating it. We're very, very clever. God has made us to be clever, and He has given us the dominion, which is all art. So a painting is art, but the wheat field is art as well. Cooking a meal is art, too. A natural meal would be to go and to eat berries from the vine. But if you bring food into a shelter and you apply fire to it, that is not natural, it is artistic. So it is impossible to be human without being artistic. Someone who says, "I am not artistic", in my view, doesn't understand what art is. He is artistic, and he should rejoice in that, and take a certain responsibility for it. He may not be a painter or a dancer or an architect or a music composer, but he is fundamentally artistic in his being and identity as God's image. We are artistic and creative, and we have dominion over the natural reality around us. That dominion can be misused in destructive ways, which is not pleasing to God, because God is greener than anybody. He wants people to use their artistic, manipulative creativity not to destroy nature, but to sustain nature.

But aren't there different categories of art? Isn't there a difference between art that is understood to feed the people and a painting that I paint just for the sake of painting it—because it is beautiful, because I express my talent?

I'm not really big on the fundamental necessity to express a talent. I think it's fine and good, and it can be a blessing, but I see that as more similar to growing wheat in a field than different. The wheat in the field is an art form. There is a beauty, symmetry, a shape. People can make beautiful wheat fields, orderly wheat fields, and they can make ugly, disorderly, sloppy wheat fields. They are not all the same. It feeds not only the body with bread, but it feeds the whole esthetic awareness of appropriateness and fittingness of shape, season, rhythm, color and texture, which are all a part of dance, painting and music.

Should art be used for worship?

The word worship means *worth-ship*, meaning attitudes and activities that proclaim and acknowledge the worth of God. We are worshipping creatures. Making a painting can be worship, but baking bread is also worship, and growing a wheat field is also worship.

In one of your writings you suggest that we need to make a checklist before going to the cinema, because we need to be responsible for giving ourselves over to watching something. Do we really have to be that careful when discerning or absorbing art—whether it's a painting, or a book by Dostoyevsky or a movie?

I think that entertainment is a good thing, and a useful therapeutic part of our life. The English word "entertainment" comes from the Latin words *inter* and *tenere*, which mean *to hold between*. So we have one active and responsible engaged part of our life, and we have another active and responsible engaged part of our life, and our entertainment is to be held between the two—to be somehow suspended, to be somehow not engaged or responsible. Entertainment is watching the squirrels playing on the trees. We are not responsible for that. The squirrels are not saying anything. There is no content, there is no idea coming from them. It's just pure joy in watching God's creation. To look at the beautiful sunset is properly entertaining. I don't think that we should use art as entertainment. Whether it is a painting, or music, or a film, or an essay, or a cartoon series on the television or on the Internet, the things that people say should be engaging and stimulating. There should be a response, and there should be a responsibility in our engagement and relationship to them. That is not necessary when we are entertained. I can see the therapeutic value of using, for instance, music to entertain, to suspend thought, to just listen and be carried away, and to visualize pink clouds in a blue sky, and relieve our stress. I can see the value in that in the same way that I can see in taking Valium or Prozac. I don't think it's wrong to take Valium or Prozac. I think it can be done wrongly, but I don't think it's fundamentally wrong to take those things as a therapy. I don't think it's wrong to use music as a drug, but if we principally use it as a drug, it's degrading and dehumanizing for us.

How should we use music instead?

We should use it as a relationship and as a conversation. We should try to hear what the music says, and respond to it. We should be engaged humanly with the music. We shouldn't treat it

MUSIC TO JUST LISTEN AND BE CARRIED AWAY, AND TO VISUALIZE PINK CLOUDS IN A BLUE SKY.

as a product. We shouldn't make the composer or the performer into a prostitute, consuming what they produce and paying for it with our money, time or attention. Instead, we should take them seriously as someone who has something to say.

On happiness and the fruits of the Spirit

You mentioned earlier that you were not particularly happy as a Zen Buddhist monk. Were you a happier person as a Christian working at L'Abri?

I'm not sure, but probably not. It depends on how you measure happiness.

Were you more fulfilled?

My life was larger, engaged in a greater variety of things. If that means fulfilled, then yes.

If happiness or fulfillment are not helpful terms, how can a Christion discern whether he or she is going in the right direction as far as following Jesus is concerned?

One can discern the growth of the fruits of the Spirit, and if the fruits of the Spirit are growing, then your life is progressing well, you are growing in the Lord, you are growing in Christlikeness. The chief value of the Kingdom of God is fruitfulness. The chief value of the kingdom of this world—where we both come from—is success. I think Christians are sometimes confused concerning those things. People interpret success as God's endorsement, or God's ratification of our obedience, or our spirituality, rather than looking for fruitfulness. In the Kingdom of God, if you don't have a lot of success, things don't work out, you don't build a big church, don't have a new radio program, or are not very influential, but you increase in the fruits of the Spirit, you are a winner. But if you do build a big church, and convert thousands, and become famous, and give your body to be burned, and you don't increase in the fruits of the Spirit, you are a loser—which in terms of the kingdom of this world is complete nonsense. I think the Bible is quite clear that these are the real values.

Did you have more peace or shalom at L'Abri then as a Zen Buddhist?

Maybe in some ways I did have a greater shalom, because I grew in more ways, which was very stressful, although the shalom of God sustained and stabilized me. The shalom is the framework, the foundation that God gives me, a rock to stand on, and a direction to orient myself toward Christ. That is the peace that stabilizes me, even when internally and in my activities and in my relationships, there might be great stress, uncertainty and conflict. The peace of God, the shalom, which passes all understanding, keeps my heart and my mind in Jesus Christ. So in that sense I had more peace, but I almost never use the word "peace", because it's generally understood as a personal lack of conflict, a feeling of safety and satisfaction. I don't think that's what shalom means.

Another fruit of the Spirit is joy. Would you say that as Christians we should have more joy in our lives?

Yes, as long as we don't equate joy with happiness. Biblical joy is connected more with peace, with wellbeing. It means that, despite my suffering and conflicts, I rejoice because I belong to God and I'm kept by Him.

Just like Paul and Silas had joy while singing in chains in the prison?

Yes.

Can a genuinely Christian person be unhappy?

Yes. I have known people who were in the process of going blind, or were single and lonely, and Christians. They were caring and serving people, they trusted God, and were not happy. I don't think the apostle Paul was a particularly cheerful person. I frankly don't think he would have been an easy person to be with. That's comforting to me, because I'm not an easy person to be with.

Are there other ways that you grew during your early years as a Christian in terms of the fruits of the Spirit?

I can think of a couple of things that are relevant. One is that I grew in the capacity to enjoy a wider variety of personality types. I knew that I was required by God to love everyone, whether I was similar or different, liked them or didn't like them.

For example, it's always been difficult for me to be with people who always make statements and never ask questions. It's difficult for me to be with people who finish my sentences for me. It's difficult for me to be with people for whom everything is a joke, and they mask and anesthetize their life with silly laughter. Those would be some examples of people that are really not naturally easy for me, although gradually I have come to be able to cope with these personality types.

In making the effort to love everyone, and in praying for that, I also found that I began to enjoy types of people and situations I had never enjoyed before. That too seemed to me to be some kind

Can a genuinely Christian person be unhappy?

of growth, and some kind of peace, and some kind of joy. I was really glad that I could do that. It made my life less tense, and more relaxed, and more at home with my environment. The process is still going on.

As we grow as Christians, how can we know if our heart is being changed in the right way?

The promise in Jeremiah and Ezekiel is that we don't have to relate to God from our heart, but that God will give us a new heart. That is a new life, a new me, a redeemed, restructured, and reoriented person. I don't think I need to work with my heart, as it is sinful, self-centered and broken, but I need to look to God to give me a new heart, a new center, a new set of references to understand who I am. My understanding of becoming more God-shaped is coming to me in a variety of ways. This would be a more epistemological question: "How do I know that I'm becoming more God-shaped and that I'm not inventing a god in my image?" In the Bible, we see how Jesus is described as a suffering servant, as other-centered, as giving His life for others, as loving others, as challenging others, as not being polite, but being real. Very often, He has actually been quite rude in being real and in challenging people, and in stimulating paradigm shifts in people's understanding. When we make choices that echo and follow that pattern of Jesus' life in relating to people, caring about people and serving people, then we can have some objective criteria for knowing that we are becoming more like Jesus. Also, I think the fruits of the Spirit are a good way to measure our spiritual temperature, as it were. If we can observe that we increase in patience, kindness, goodness, gentleness, faithfulness and self-control, then that is a clear evidence that I have life in Christ and that I'm becoming more like Christ, that I am becoming God-shaped, that I am becoming more fully, clearly and functionally the image of God.

A lot of people have developed sophisticated programs for becoming a Christian—four steps, five steps, eight steps, and so on. Have you ever considered the possibility of developing an Ellis Potter methodology?

I don't much believe in methodologies, or in methods for evangelism or apologetics. I think people need to be taken as they are, and that we need to shape our caring for them, and serve them with truth on a moment-by-moment basis. We cannot accurately predict how people will react and what stages they will go through in their life. I think we have to take it as it comes.

On books, writing and sermons

Besides Francis Schaeffer, who were the other writers, thinkers, and theologians who shaped your thinking?

Examples would include Harry Blamires, N.T. Wright, and F.F. Bruce. I would also say George Bernard Shaw has shaped my thinking and my communications, especially reading his collected music criticisms, which are in three volumes. They are well over a thousand pages and I read them twice. I think they were a bit formative in ways of analysis, observation and expression. I also learned clarity and concision of expression from Shaw. Another writer I've learned from is Sir Thomas Malory, who wrote *The Death of Arthur*. I love the eloquence, the grandeur of his expressions, and I think they've influenced the way I teach. I read widely in variety of genres, and believe that everything I read shapes my thinking in some ways, at least temporarily.

Do you read any fiction?

I have read a lot of fiction over the years, from Cervantes' *Don Quixote* to contemporary novels. Good fiction writers are perceptive and expressive artists, whether Christian or not. They give an insight into various cultures and periods of history and show us ourselves, sometimes in uncomfortable ways. My wife and I started a mission behind the Iron Curtain and read lots of fiction coming from the Soviet Empire countries, some of which was smuggled out to the West for publication. This was a great help in understanding the attitudes and experiences of the people we were trying to serve. I also read a lot of science fiction. Much science fiction is basically atheistic but also astonishingly prophetic in terms of technology and ethics. If you want to know how the non-Christian mind works, read a lot of science fiction.

What are the books you haven't written yet, but you would like to write?

There is a book in draft form of a series of sermons on the letter of James. Also, in addition to my book *3 Theories of Everything* on comparative worldviews, and *How Do You Know That?* on epistemology, I will be writing a book on spirituality. I would like to do more books of collected sermons. There is also a manuscript of partly edited transcriptions of L'Abri conversations from 1983 and 1984, which I would very much like to make into a book.

How do you prepare your sermons?

I print out a section of the Bible text with large spaces between the lines. In the spaces, I put in Greek or Hebrew notations in pencil. Then I add cross-references and notes in ink, and I preach from that. My notes are minimalistic. I never prepare my sermons as a manuscript. The notes that I make usually have more content than can be delivered in the length of a sermon. I know before I get into the pulpit that I won't say everything that I had thought of saying. The sermon will need to be edited while delivering it. I pray fervently that the Holy Spirit will edit the text which doesn't actually exist yet, so that it speaks to the people and makes a whole sermon. Usually, I am motivated to leave out some things that I have put in the notes. Sometimes I don't see them. I just have a blind spot, and afterwards I might realize, "Oh, I forgot to say that!", and I think, "Well, was it really necessary, or do I need to say it next time?" Usually it would not have belonged well in the sermon. Also, things come to me while I preach that are not in the notes, and I say those things. Last Sunday, I preached on the first part of Chapter 2 of Titus, and my notes looked like a shorter-than-average sermon. My average sermon is between thirty to thirty-five minutes, and this looked like twenty-five minutes, but it turned out to be forty-five minutes, and there was no fluff. It was content, content, content and illustrations, and applications and examples that came to me as I preached. So I don't make a beautiful eloquent sermon—I put ideas together and cross-references, and I have a basic picture of what the text says and how it relates to other passages in the Bible and how it connects to the people that I'm preaching to. I also understand and try to point out how the text has sometimes been interpreted badly. So, I have notes on paper, but I don't know what the sermon will actually sound like until I hear a recording of it.

The twenty hours that you spend preparing for sermons involves researching the Bible, praying about it, reading commentaries—those sorts of activities?
Yes.

Is it similar with your lectures?
A bit less. Lectures have fairly minimal notes, but my lectures are more similar each time I give them. It's interesting that if I preach a sermon three or four times, it gets shorter and more content-full. There is more in it, but it takes less time to deliver it, and it's clearer. It flows together more tightly.

3 Theories of Everything is a really wonderful book. Was it difficult to write?

I didn't write *3 Theories*.

Who wrote it?

Peco Gaskovski.

Okay.

He is my editor. The process—and it was the same with *How Do You Know That?*—was that several recordings of the lecture were transcribed and collated, with the repetitions taken out. It was very laborious. That collation was the rough draft, and then it was edited and processed. We talked about it and took things out, put things in, and so on.

So, had it not been for an editor you wouldn't have written or published a book?

Most likely not. My editor has mentioned that it was actually his wife who repeatedly urged him to urge me that we should write a book, so it also might not have happened if it weren't for her insistence.

In 3 Theories you remarked that non-believers often understand you better than believers. Is this a compliment to non-believers or a criticism of believers?

I'm not given to making compliments, and I try hard not to flatter people. I try to speak the truth, and so sometimes I tell people, "You are very intelligent." And they say, "Thank you." And I say, "Oh, no, it's not a compliment, it's just an observation. It's not your fault. I'm not praising you; I'm just saying you're very intelligent. It must be a burden to have that much intelligence. You're responsible for using it—that's one of the conditions of your life. I'm not saying that you earned it or produced it or something like that." So yes, I'm not in the habit of complimenting people. For the most part I just say what I observe.

As for believers versus non-believers, there can be differences in their thinking habits. Sometimes people who are religious and who are involved in a community of people who have similar faith experiences, principles and practices can become "true believers". By this, I mean that their mind is made up, and they don't want to be confused with the facts. By the same token, many Christians—but not only Christians—develop a jargon with particular code words, or *shibboleths*. A shibboleth is a word that has to be said in a precise way, or a series of words that has to be exactly in a precise order, or the person is not acceptable. I find that Christians have a tendency to do this. They expect to hear certain phrases. When I preached in Basel regularly, I gave note sheets to the people with three major points. On the sheet was also a blank space they could fill in with what they had learned. Sometimes I saw people's note sheets, and I observed that they mostly wrote down things they already knew. New things that I said, that I hoped they would learn, didn't make it into their notes. New angles, new nuances, didn't make it into the thinking process of these quite intelligent people. I find that that is often the case with Christians in an audience that I'm speaking to. Non-Christians come more *tabula rasa*—as a clean slate. They don't know the jargon, don't have expectations, don't have a grid to put me in, and they're more open and receptive to what I say. When I say something that is not in the traditional, customary way of how evangelical Christians speak, the non-Christians are not disturbed at all; they take it at face value and deal with it. Christians are a bit disturbed, because "that's not the way it is supposed to be said". So, yes, it seems to me that the thinking habits of Christians could improve.

On escapism and Heaven

What have been some of your most important realizations and theological discoveries throughout the years?

It was a very important realization that the Kingdom of Heaven is coming, and it will come fully into the creation. This means that we will not go to it, which is most commonly believed. The Christian goal is not escape. The Christian goal and hope is engagement. There are a lot of people who are strongly motivated toward escape. The biblical teaching about redemption will be realized on the earth and not someplace else. Redemption is from the values of this world, not from the world itself, because God made the world and loves it. We are taught to be in the world but not of the world. In some ways, many Christians have lived out of the world, but of the world. They formed their own isolated communities, but they lived by the values of the world—success, fulfillment, enjoyment, and these kinds of things.

The world is the salt and the light of the church. Platonic transcendentalism and Gnosticism came into the church early on. These views reflect the basic belief that the transcendent is more real than the actual. They support the "pie in the sky when you die by and by" form of Christianity, as well as attitudes and practices that can make Christians "so heavenly minded they are of no earthly use". The writers of the New Testament letters were all fighting against Platonism and Proto-Gnosticism. I think that the apostles lost the fight. Platonism and Gnosticism have been alive and well in the church in every generation for the last two thousand years. We still need to fight the fight.

What signs of escapism do you see in today's church?

I see a bit less now, but it's still present. In the last thirty or forty years, in the evangelical church, there has been a strong attraction to thinking about the rapture. All of that was grounded on one verse in Thessalonians—and they misinterpreted that verse. The verse is, "The Lord Himself will descend from heaven...and first those who are dead in Christ will rise, and then those of us who remain will rise to meet him in the air." The escapist rapture-interpretation of that is that we meet Him in the air so that He can take us someplace else. But that is not what it means. The word "meet" that Paul uses is the word that was used for the governors of a city or a country coming out of the city to meet the emperor when he came to visit, in order to accompany him into the city. It was the same word used when the Christians came from Rome to *Three Taverns* to meet Paul—not to go back to Malta with Paul, but to accompany him on his journey to Rome. When Jesus appears, the believers will rise to meet him in the air to accompany Him onto the earth where He is coming and will be forever. So Christians will not be taken by Him to someplace else, which is most commonly believed by Christians all over the world. Most Christians believe that the goal of the Christian life is to go to heaven when you die, but that is not the biblical picture. The goal of Christians is to be fully engaged in the creation with God forever, and not go someplace else. The word *telos* appears in the Bible to refer to this goal, but it's been difficult in some languages to translate *telos*. For instance, in English it is often understood as not only the goal or the arrival, but as the "finish". Hence the following phrase, popularly associated with the Bible: "The end is near."

The Greek says the *telos* is near—meaning the goal is near. People assume that the "end" means that the world is going to be burnt up, finished, thrown away, given to the devil, and God is going to take all His people someplace else. But *telos* means that the goal is near, and the goal is the redemption of the creation and the appearing of the Lord in the creation. So, it actually means that the *beginning* is near—the beginning of the new heaven and new earth, the beginning of the new administration of the Kingdom of God. Most Christians have understood this to mean that the goal is the end, but the goal is not the end, it is the beginning! That's been an important concept to me, and partly because of that, I'm in the process of writing a lecture called *God is Green*.

By "green" you mean…?

I mean ecologically sound, ecologically motivated, ecologically concerned and engaged. This is something that I've said to Greenpeace people when I meet with them in the street: "You know, nobody is greener than God." God made the green, and He loves it, but Christians have traditionally not known that. Christians have believed that God is brown, and that He's going to burn up the earth, and that the earth and our bodies and our society and our creativity have no value. It's only some supernaturally connected part of us, which is mistakenly called the soul, that has value. This is not really the message of Christianity.

You see, most people, Christians and non-Christians alike, believe that people have a soul, but biblically that's not true. People *are* souls. A friend of mine who works in L'Abri asked me a few months ago what I thought the soul was, and I said the soul is the glue that holds the different parts of us together. So you have your body, your mind, your emotions, your will, your creativity, your relationships—these are all ingredients of who you are as a person. Your soul is the glue that holds them all together. If you lose your soul, you lose your glue—you fall apart and you die. The soul is not a little glowing thing that's inside of you! That would more accurately be described as the spirit, although it wouldn't be an adequate description of the spirit either, because spirit means "wind". It's what goes out from you, and your soul is your glue, the integrity of the bundle of the bits that go together to make who you are. Your soul will be with God forever, which means your body, your mind, your creativity, all of these things. Most people think that the goal of Christianity is to be some sort of semi-transparent disembodied transcendental entity that lives a completely other kind of existence sitting on clouds and playing harps and wearing wings. That sounds like hell to me. It's just utterly boring. The Bible doesn't give us that. It gives us full engagement in the redeemed creation with God.

So what happens when we die?

When we die our spirit goes to be with Jesus, who is here, but in other dimensions of reality. He is not appearing presently, but He has promised, "I am with you until the end of the age", so He is not someplace else. He went, and He didn't go. He ascended not into the sky, but into the cloud, into the interface between the created and uncreated dimensions of reality. He ascended not to another place, but into other dimensions, and He is immediately with us coextensive with the space that we experience. So we don't have to shout in order for Him to hear us. He is right here, but we don't see Him, and He will appear like lightning over the whole earth with judgment. Judgment, by the way, means to make right, to justify, to rectify, to make things to be as they should be, and not only to condemn. When we die, we are in the presence of God and Christ and the Holy Spirit, and we know it, but there is a frustrated longing and waiting for the full redemption of our new bodies. In the Book of Revelation, the saints under the altar are crying out for the final reality to be realized. There is no dread or anxiety or confusion, because people who die in the Lord will know that they are in the Lord and belong with the Lord. They are with the Lord in a very real sense, and at the same time waiting for their new bodies and the redemption of the creation.

What happens to the soul when we die?

The soul is incomplete when we die, and it waits to be made complete again, when there is a new body.

On suffering and emotions

A lot of Christians struggle with the reality of pain. What are your experiences in responding to people's pain?

As a pastor a lot of people come to me with a passionate cry: "Why did something bad happen? Why am I confused? Why did I lose my job? Why did I break my leg?" They don't understand, and they suffer from not understanding, because they feel that they should understand. Many of them feel that somehow God owes them an explanation. This is not a good attitude, but it's not surprising. When I teach about this, I often tell people a fictitious scenario about myself. I'm a missionary and I travel, so let us picture me on a missionary journey. Suppose I need to catch a train, and I am late and running to get on the train, and I slip on a banana peel and break my ankle. Then, as I lie on the platform and watch the train pulling out of the station, I might ask, "Why did this happen to me?" The answer could be that it is the result of my sin in getting up late, or it could be the result of the sin of the banana-eater throwing the peel on the platform. Or, it could have been caused by the devil, because people would have been blessed where I go, or it could have been caused by God, because the train was going to crash down the track and He didn't want me to be on it. My peace and joy doesn't depend on my figuring out why this happened. Romans 8:28 tell us, "All things"—including broken ankles—"work for good for those that love the Lord." So the question should not be "Why?" but rather "Do I love the Lord?" The biblical statement is clear. If I love the Lord, then this broken ankle will be caused to work for good. I might end up talking to a nurse or an elderly person at the hospital and be a blessing to them, or I might learn patience, or I might be saved from my workaholism—or something else. Various good things can happen that I just don't know about in advance. We walk by faith and not by sight, so we don't always see the "why" in the past, just like we don't see how it will work for good in the future.

Do you have an opinion about how helpful or unhelpful our emotions are with regard to experiencing God?

I think our emotions, when they happen to us, are morally neutral. But we need to respond to them in moral, ethical, and faithful ways, and we should never trust them, because they sometimes lie. Not always, but often. Therefore, we shouldn't take our emotions as guidance or revelation or truth or fact. They're real, but usually they don't teach us much. They can teach us something about ourselves and that can be valuable. But my reaction to a broken ankle, whether it is hope or resignation or fear or anger or disappointment, is like the weather. It just happens to me and I don't learn much from the changing weather about my relationship to God or my identity in Christ. The emotions that happen to me are largely morally neutral and I'm not responsible for them. If anger happens, I'm not responsible for it happening. The anger happening is a temptation, but I'm not guilty of my temptations, I'm guilty of my choices. So I have the temptation of anger, and then I have to make a choice about it. Do I follow the anger? Do I feed the anger? Do I wallow in the anger? Do I act on the anger? Or do I put the anger in context and realize that it shouldn't be the only emotion or the only impression that's going on? For that I am responsible, not for the occurrence of the anger. I'm not to be praised or blamed for that. The emotion just happens.

It's like the weather. It just happens to me and I don't learn very much from the changing weather about my relationship to God.

In many churches one gets the impression that there is almost a plan for the church service: "How can we best induce good emotions with our worship?" Where would you draw the line? How much should we seek emotions and how should they be integrated in the church service?

I don't really believe in drawing lines. I think if you draw a line you're going to sit down on it and die. I think we should leave things a bit more fluid. When you draw a line, you tend to fall asleep, and assume, "I've done that, and I don't have to think about it anymore." We always need to think about these things, because circumstances change, the people involved in the church change, the weather changes, all kinds of things change. That means we need to adjust with it and not just have a line, and to say this line was given to us by God, by the Holy Spirit, and it shall not move. We have to be careful not to do that, but to stay awake and to ask, "What are we doing?" In the context of strong emotions, it is difficult to ask questions, because strong emotions make it difficult to think. Not that they are wrong, but they need to be contextualized with reason and thought. We talked about smoking marijuana before, and I think this is fairly similar. When one smokes marijuana, one concentrates and focuses on something and sees it in great detail and sharply. We have a sensation of being very intelligent, aware and perceptive. In a sense that is true, but in a sense we become quite stupid, because our field of vision becomes narrow, our awareness of reality becomes small. When we have—especially in groups and particularly in large groups—strong emotions, our life actually becomes smaller. It feels rich, it feels overflowing, it feels really good and lively, but I think there is actually less life. When the emotion fills the whole screen of what we

see in our life and thought and relationships, and other kinds of awareness are pushed aside by the emotion, we just have the trip of the emotion. I don't think that's wrong, but it's a mistake to let those kinds of experiences guide us in decision-making. I often go to Pentecostal, charismatic churches to preach, and I have a lot of charismatic friends. In some of these churches people have the idea that there will be an evening meeting—the band will start at 7 o'clock, and people will start to sing and clap and dance, and by 7:30 the Holy Spirit will be there. This is shamanism! This is not Christianity, because you cannot control the Holy Spirit. If the Holy Spirit is in you, you will burst into tears and shout on the bus going to work in the morning. If you suddenly begin to speak in tongues waiting in line at the bank, that's probably the Holy Spirit.

Are you willing to work in the context that you call shamanism?

Yes. I go and I teach, and often I teach directly against something that's going on at the time. Usually, the people are friendly and they hear my teaching, and invite me back, which I think is a work of the Holy Spirit. I cannot remember going to a Pentecostal or charismatic church where I was not blessed, in the sense of my life being enlarged and enriched.

If you suddenly begin to speak in tongues waiting in line at the bank, that's probably the Holy Spirit.
ДАВАЙ ДАВАЙ
(GIVE, GIVE)
KASSZA
(CASSIER)

On apologetics

I recall you once lectured on "apologetics as love". A lot of people that I know, when they think about apologetics, don't necessarily think about love or they reframe the word "love" as "tough love". How can we genuinely talk about our faith and express love at the same time?

I'm not fond of the word "apologetics". I use the word "kategorics" instead. Apologetics means defense, and the great commission is not, "Go into all the world and defend yourselves." The defense can turn into attack, and the function of apologetics is sometimes to win and to defeat. I find that a bit counterproductive. *Kategoria* as opposed to *apologia* is to give the categories of reality, as in the ancient Greek court system. The prosecutor gave the categories of crime—the dead body, the motive, the knife, the witnesses. The apologia might claim that, "the witnesses were drunk and they're liars", and "that's not my knife, and I didn't even know this guy". The mantra of Christian apologetics is 1 Peter 3:15: "Always be prepared to give an answer to those who question the faith that is in you" (and do this with gentleness and respect). I believe that instruction is from the Holy Spirit, and that we should take it seriously. The difficulty is that no one is asking. I should be prepared to give an answer, but no one is questioning the faith that is in me, because nobody cares. The kategoria are pre-apologetics, involving giving the categories that stimulate the useful questions that people can ask about the faith that is in me. Serving the people with the questions that will be useful to them is love.

Do you see a clear and present danger of syncretism in our culture today, in the sense of people taking bits and pieces from different religions in order to better accommodate to their own tastes?

I think there is a real and present danger of it in every culture and in every period in history—perhaps more, perhaps less, depending on the culture. In smaller, more isolated cultures there might be less danger of syncretism, because there isn't an awareness of the variety of points of view and practices. In a strongly traditional culture, what people already know now is probably all that they will know. In a cosmopolitan situation there is a greater danger of mixing things up, watering them down, or confusing them. The opposite of syncretism, which is fanaticism, is also a danger. We can become the "frozen chosen" and unteachable. I think both are dangers, and that we need to guard against both extremes. We are not fully capable of precisely finding the middle path, walking the narrow road between. We really need God to guide us in that, and I think the path, although Jesus described it as narrow, is not a thread. We don't have to walk single file necessarily. We could walk side by side—and if I walk by your side, I'm not walking in your footsteps. We can walk side by side and we can both walk in the footsteps of Jesus and be on the narrow path.

On words

Words and definitions seem to matter to you greatly. Can tell me more about that?

I tend not to argue over words, but to ask people what they mean. I find that often people have almost no idea what they mean. This is frightening, and I think people should be frightened when they don't know what they mean when they use words. They use words because they have an aura, or a sensation, or an association, but they really are not responsible for the language that they use.

And you want to make them feel responsible?

It's not so important that people feel responsible, but that they are responsible. I believe that I bless them by inviting them to be genuine and responsible for the language that they use. I believe that just nodding my head and saying, "Aha, aha", is not helpful to people. It's not that I always insist on using the dictionary definition. If someone has a clear idea of what they mean by a word and it's quite different from the dictionary definition, I accept it as what they mean. I just want to know what they mean. Often, people do not know what they mean. They're just floating around and using slogan words that they've read or heard in the press or seen on television, and they don't know what they're saying. Increasingly, in postmodern society, people's attitude about words is "whatever". Imagine a postmodern wedding in which the pastor says, "George, do you take Emily to be your lawfully wedded wife to have and to hold, to cherish in sickness and in health, for richer or poorer till death do you part?", and George says "Whatever. It's all good." That doesn't do. We need him to say, "Yes." "Whatever" is not sufficient. It's nothing you can hold or stand on, nothing solid as a foundation or framework for life. It's slippery and it gives excessive freedom. In the postmodern world, freedom is the highest value. In reality, total freedom always equals death. Freedom without form is death; the death of language, the death of the person, the death of relationships. The worship of freedom is a culture of death. We are living in a world where that religion is prominent. It is a battle, and we need to do our part. We need to make an effort to bless people, and to shout "Fire!" when the building is on fire. We need to say, "We're losing our language!"

The first thing we know about God is that He speaks, and His speech has meaning, and is definite. It's not a "whatever" kind of speech. He wants us to be in His image, which includes speaking. The first thing Adam did in becoming the image of God was to speak, to name the animals. He named them cow, horse, pig, cat. He didn't say "whatever", "sort of", "maybe". If we lose our language and meaning, we lose the Bible. In discussing what passages in the Bible mean, when the discussion gets difficult, people sometimes say: "It's only words..." This is death. It's only words? *Whatever! Let's smile at each other, let's be authentic!* God does matter, because God speaks, and they're not only words, they are The Word of God. The Word of God is not "whatever". It's hot or cold, and we must be hot or cold. If we're lukewarm, He will spit us out of His mouth. So as I deal with people, I try to encourage them to be hot or cold. Not in terms of the dictionary, but in terms of their own genuineness and commitment to the language that they use. I am committed to say, "Yes, I mean this", and the meaning is not floating around so that I'm not responsible for it. I am responsible. I say this, and I mean this, and if I'm wrong, I need to be shown that I'm wrong. But I believe I'm right, so I say it. Increasingly, that isn't how people use language. They use it emotionally for flavor, for atmosphere, and that is not all of what language is for. I believe this is important. In my work, I try as hard as I can to encourage people to treasure language and to be responsible for it, to use it in a godly and not in a manipulative or atmospheric way. The latter is a huge temptation. I am sympathetic about the temptation, but I don't feel that I can encourage people in following it.

Final thoughts

We have talked about your childhood, your life as a seeker and a Buddhist monk, your life at L'Abri, your life as a pastor, and now as a part-time pastor and independent missionary. So far, which period of your life was the most formative?

My parent's divorce was quite formative in that I'm an insecure person. I have a fear of abandonment, and I need community and stability. I actively dislike change. Sometimes I accept it cheerfully, and I can see logically why the change is right, but I never like it. I think those parts of who I am were formed in my first two years of life. This form of who I am is broken, because I'm a sinner and a broken person, and because events in my life have broken me in various ways. My formation is a distorted structure with pieces missing and lopsided. Things need to be propped up and compensated for. My formation is not a glorious story of how I blossomed like a flower. I'm a saved wretch. I'm a wretch, but I'm God's wretch, so I'm confident that I will always be God's, and eventually I won't be a wretch anymore.

It was also formative to be with my family when I had a brother and a sister—I learned a lot from that. Then it was formative to be a Zen Buddhist, and also to be involved in all of these other movements. All of that helped to form my thinking process and my search for absolutes. I tend to cut through peripheral issues and ask, "So what? Does this contribute to arriving at a conclusion or a point?"

Being married was also formative in my life. It taught me patience, loyalty and acceptance of a greater variety of circumstances and behaviors. My time at L'Abri was formative in teaching me to teach and preach, and many other things. One day someone asked me what was the favorite part of my work at L'Abri. Without any thought, I said, "Preaching." Then I went away and asked myself, *Why did I say that? Is that true?* I thought about it carefully and I realized, *Yes, it is true.* It was the favorite part of my life, and it still is. It's the most frightening thing that I do, but it's my favorite thing. My preaching skills further developed in my years as a pastor. Those years formed in me a capacity to ignore things that are not essential. I learned not to concentrate on fixing everything all the time. To some extent, it healed me of my perfectionism. That healing process is still continuing.

Is there anything that you would do differently in your life, if you could?

Millions of things. Almost everything I've ever done could possibly have been done better, but I chose what I chose and I did what I did. I live in the consequences of those things, and other people also live in the consequences. I cannot go back in history and change things. I know there are ways that I have hurt, disappointed and confused people, and I'm sorry about that. But I cannot undo those things, although I can be forgiven, and in some cases make things better.

What is the legacy you would like to leave behind? How would you like people to remember you?

I would like people to remember Jesus. I don't feel strongly that I need to be remembered. I've started to publish books, and so my name will be on those books, and after I'm dead, the books will probably still be alive. I would be glad if my work, my books, and my lectures continued to be a blessing after I die. In first Thessalonians, at the end of chapter two, Paul wrote that "the hope, joy, and crown" in which he would glory, is other people whom he has blessed. I would like my legacy to be the beautified lives of other people.

About Ellis Potter

Ellis Potter, a native Californian now residing in Switzerland, is a former Buddhist monk who became a Christian in 1976 under the influence and ministry of the late Dr. Francis Schaeffer.

After his conversion, Mr. Potter worked on the staff of L'Abri Fellowship until 1991. L'Abri Fellowship is an evangelical residential study community, founded by Dr. Schaeffer. Students of all ages, backgrounds and nationalities come to the fellowship with reasons as diverse as the students themselves. At L'Abri, all questions are taken seriously and respected, and biblical answers to life's complexities are offered. As a worker at L'Abri for many years, Mr. Potter counseled, lectured, taught and encouraged hundreds of students from all over the world.

Mr. Potter's unique background includes music, the arts, theology and philosophy. He lectures internationally on a variety of subjects, including the relevancy of Christianity to the arts and modern philosophical and social movements. He often lectures on a comparison of biblical and other worldviews, seeking to establish the clear truth of God's Word, and to encourage people's trust in it. He has traveled extensively on all five continents for teaching and preaching in churches, camps, conferences and universities.

Along with lecturing, Mr. Potter has pastored at several English-speaking churches in Switzerland. He also works as an independent missionary, directing most of his attention and energies eastward to various nations in Central and Eastern Europe.

Lightning Source UK Ltd.
Milton Keynes UK
UKHW03f2000100418
320825UK00001B/26/P